Discoveries

BOOKS BY EUGENIA PRICE . . .

Discoveries – Made from Living My New Life

Never a Dull Moment

Share My Pleasant Stones

Early Will I Seek Thee

The Burden Is Light

What Is God Like?

Beloved World

A Woman's Choice

Find Out for Yourself

God Speaks to Women Today

Woman to Woman

Just As I Am

The Wider Place

Make Love Your Aim

The Unique World of Women

Learning to Live From the Gospels

The Beloved Invader

New Moon Rising

EUGENIA PRICE

Discoveries
Made From Living My New Life

New Revised Edition

Zondervan Publishing House
Grand Rapids, Michigan

Discoveries

Zondervan Publishing House
Grand Rapids, Michigan

First printing of Revised Edition. . . .1970

Printed in the United States of America

TO

Ellen Riley Urquhart

. . . the one through whom He found me

Preface

Sometime ago a friend said, "You should read your first book *Discoveries* – it will do you good!"

It has.

And I am interested to see that after nearly twenty years, I have come almost full circle in my thinking about the Christian life. From my tenth book, *What Is God Like,* through my fifteenth, *Just As I Am* – my one central emphasis has been exactly what it was in this my very first book: Jesus Christ Himself. Not that He hasn't *seemed* central to me all along. He has, but as with anyone on a spiritual journey, new truths about the central issue can capture an author's attention for one book and another. This, of course, is the risk involved in permitting one's discoveries to be set in type. Almost never does a writer have the opportunity my friends at Zondervan Publishing House have given me here. I am being allowed to update in any way I like the first book I ever wrote.

After rereading it carefully and chuckling at some of the very "young" sounds in it, I find that most of what few changes I have made involve only sentence structure and the scooping out of handsful of exclamation points. In those first days of my new life in Christ everything was exclamatory.

I confess to feeling that way still, but I have learned, I hope, some literary discipline.

I confess that certain flat, sweeping statements have a glib ring to me now — almost amusing, as one is naturally amused at a child. I was a child in the kingdom of God when I wrote *Discoveries.* For the most part it was written during my second and third years as a follower of Jesus Christ. But in spite of the touches of glibness, which were left as written, I have been more amazed than amused to find how much He had taught me in so short a time. Unavoidably, when I see here in black and white that I had the basics straight from the beginning, I cringe that I have not taken more advantage through the years of what I learned so soon. Still, none of us ever grows as rapidly or as deeply as he could and so I marvel that the Holy Spirit has kept my perspective as simple and direct as my later books show it to be. Twenty years later, Christianity is still Jesus Christ to me. Not theories about Him — but the Man-God Himself. I am still His and He is still mine. To me to live is still — Jesus Christ.

As subjective as this sounds, I can see in retrospect that He has never permitted me to turn *inward* for long at a time. When I moved away from a metropolitan center to a small island, many of my self-appointed "spiritual monitors" decided at once that I was entering a period of unhealthy, indulgent hibernation. I did withdraw from crowds of people, but merely because I was determined to find myself as just another member of the human race — alone with God. I didn't know it then — but I certainly know now — that God's people push new Christians out onto platforms and into adoring crowds far too fast. For twelve years I had traveled from one church to another, from one woman's retreat to another, from one campus to another — being, as I honestly thought when I wrote *Discoveries* — the right kind of "spiritual doormat." The time came when God's voice sounded more clearly than the insistent speaking requests and I called a halt, moved to new surroundings and began to learn how to *live* the Christian life *in community* with people. The same people week in and week out. Warm hearted, somewhat provincial folk in the main, who don't love me or accept me merely because I write books – but for myself. People who do not hold me responsible for answers, who do not scrutinize the way I dress or enjoy myself. People who have permitted me to become a part of the landscape as I so longed to do.

During these more normal years, instead of turning *inward,* as was predicted, I have found myself turning almost entirely *outward.* I am involved in community activity as I never dreamed I'd be. I am learning to shed my prejudices in the context of day to day relationships, how to see problems through to a solution instead of tossing off a word of hasty counsel before hopping a plane for the next speaking engagement. I have learned the wisdom of being honest – of saying what is true, rather than what will make me seem wise or the hearer happy. Hopefully, I have almost learned when to say nothing at all.

God, through Jesus Christ, has never been so real to me. The necessity for more and more knowledge of Him never so urgent. What I saw with almost total *subjectivity* in *Discoveries* (normal for the new Christian), I now see more *objectively.* I try to be available when there is need, but I have learned that when "doormats" are overused, they only track things up! This learning is not due to my own wisdom. It is simply the wisdom of God which He promised to give to anyone who bothered to ask for it. More than ever in my life, I am aware that *everything I have,* I have been given.

If my later books sound less glib (and I hope they do), it is not because my basic thinking has changed. It is rather, that I have had the years between in which to learn at least some respect for the complexity of human nature – including my own. I cannot help every type of person. No one can. And so, I have stopped being the harmful kind of "doormat" and don't try. This, of course, has brought the emotional maturity that comes when one is willing to be misunderstood.

Perhaps I should say here that after rereading the chapter called *Adventure in Holiness,* I decided to leave it in even though it has been wildly misinterpreted by many people. I have deep respect for anyone who speaks in tongues, but this is not what happened to me on that long ago trip to the farming section of Illinois. What happened was a meaningful, permanent deepening of my inner life with the Holy Spirit of God. In other circumstances and at several different times, such experiences have happened since. I expect them to go on happening. This is the normal way. I still hold no specific doctrinal patterns for God to follow. God is God and I am I and whatever He has or has not for me is fine.

Discoveries is a random book — written more to relieve an overflow of joy and energy during those first three years, than for publication. I am still the more surprised that after seventeen years it is not only still in print but that my publisher wants to reset the type, give it a new design, binding and jacket and offer me this opportunity to write a new, enlarged preface from the perspective of the years. It is a collection, rather than a planned book — almost every piece scratched out on a train or a plane. In many ways it is an uneven book, but for this very reason it is an authentic journal of what it was like for one so newly plunged into the wonders and the complexities and the light of the new life in Christ.

It contains the one truth which, twenty years later, is still so fresh and important and engrossing to me that I marvel to find it in these pages. A truth so all inclusive that it seems this minute to be a new discovery: *The continuing necessity for finding out more and more of what Jesus Christ is really like.* Experientially, this shining central truth seemed to become clear to me only in a much later book, *What Is God Like.* From that point on in my writing, it ties together almost everything I have to say. And yet here it is in *Discoveries.* This, I suppose, simply proves that all truth pertaining to Christ is so many-faceted, so many-dimensioned and so eternal as to be always just dawning on the finite human mind.

I am most grateful to Robert K. DeVries, Director of Publications at Zondervan Publishing House, not only for the impetus to restudy my first book about Jesus Christ, but for the initial idea of giving *Discoveries* Made From Living My New Life – this new life.

EUGENIA PRICE

St. Simons Island, Georgia

Contents

Discoveries

Concerning
Discipleship

1.

His Viewpoint or Mine?

I WAS LED INTO a personal walk with Jesus Christ by a disciple of Jesus Christ, who immediately set about fulfilling the command of her Lord, to make a disciple of me.

Jesus did not say, just before He went to sit at the right hand of the Father, "Go and save men." He said: "Go and make *disciples* of men." As I see it, a disciple is simply one who learns. One who puts himself in position to learn, and above all, one who is *willing* to learn. Does that include us? Are we in position to learn about Him? Or are we locked up, bolted down within the rigid confines of our own creed and unable to see beyond it into the breath-taking distances of God? Are we devoted to the task of bringing others into a personal relationship with Jesus Christ? Or are we bound and determined to bring them into agreement with ourselves?

Jesus said: "When the Spirit of truth comes, He will guide you into all the truth." Do we really trust the Spirit of truth or do we merely trust what *we* understand *about* Him?

Are we dogmatic *clingers* to our doctrines? Or are we *held* in the everlasting arms of Him who promised that He would never leave us nor forsake us? Are we believers in the things we know *about* Jesus Christ? Or are we believers *in* Jesus Christ Himself? Are we disciples? Are we learners? *Are* we?

What does it mean to be a disciple? Quite simply, from my own experience and from having been privileged to watch a few of God's real disciples live their daily lives, I would venture to say that if one is to become a disciple of Jesus Christ, one *must* have the *viewpoint* of Jesus Christ.

Viewpoint is a noun meaning point of view. When we look at the definition of the word "view," doors begin to open in our minds. Our "view" is widened. If we carry the definition of a disciple as one who has the viewpoint of Christ into Webster's rather complete defining of the word "view," one horizon after another collapses and we see out and away into still more of the distances of God.

First of all, "view" means the "very act of seeing." *Do we see what Christ sees in the people around us?*

Secondly, "view" means "a mental survey; a just view of the arguments." *Do we have Christ's "just view" of the arguments (rational and irrational), which we hear going on about us even among Christians?*

Thirdly, Mr. Webster says that "view" means "power of seeing; reach or range of sight." Do we have Christ's "power of seeing" those whom He sends us to help? *Do we have His "range of sight" into their needs and the causes of their separation from Him?*

Mr. Webster further defines the word "view" as "mode of looking at anything; judgment; as to state one's view of policy." Do we look through the eyes of Christ at His sheep and their predicaments? Or do we judge for ourselves as we scoff and condemn silently, the while we deceive even ourselves into believing we are leaving the judgment to Him? And the last half of that particular definition of the word "view" embraces the stating of one's view of a policy. How

Christlike are we in our view of our Christian brother's policy when it happens to disagree with our own?

"Viewpoint": a commonly used word with uncommon depths of meaning when we as believers in Jesus Christ dare to examine our own discipleship in the light of whether or not *we* live and operate from the viewpoint of the One in whom we believe.

For the next few pages we are going to go into some of the implications of having the viewpoint of Christ. Again, I confess to sharing my brand-new understanding of these things. Perhaps the reader's years of experience in walking with God will far overshadow my recent entrance into the brightness of the life for which we were born. But no matter how new the Christian follower, Jesus Christ *was* "in the beginning." And His viewpoint has and always will be without variation. For He is the rock on which our every premise may rest, and from which we may safely project our flights of understanding. If our discoveries are real and if they are true, they will return to rest upon the rock. They will be checked and re-checked and directed and patiently re-directed by the Spirit of truth who, thank God, *has* come and does dwell within us if we believe.

I believe. I have given myself over to Him. He is mine and I am His. I want to share with you what I feel He is teaching me concerning true discipleship. I want to confess my stumblings and share with you my victories and rejoice the while in the Lord, whom to know is life eternal; whom to know is to belong to and to love – forever.

2.

No Condemnation

We have dwelt at some length on what it means to have the viewpoint of Jesus Christ. We stated that it is impossible for a Christian to be a true disciple unless he possesses the viewpoint of Christ as his own. I have found this to be invariably true of my own personal life. Unless we view a dilemma in another's life as Christ views it, we are not able to help that person to a lasting solution of the problem. Unless we face the problems that arise in our life from the viewpoint of the One who has redeemed us, we do not find their workable solutions.

But even more important than seeing *problems* from the viewpoint of Christ is the absolute necessity of looking at other *people* – whether believers or non-believers – as Jesus Christ looks at them. To do this, *we* must stay out of the picture completely. With mere *human* perception, no matter how educated or how keen that perception, we simply *cannot* see others as Jesus Christ sees them. We see them smudged by our own shortcomings. We see them cracked and splintered around the edges because too often we look from the viewpoint of self-justification, especially if we happen not to have been burdened with one of the particular faults or sins under which our neighbors labor. We see them bent and shapeless because they happen to have fallen into a particular pit which, by the grace of God, we passed over.

Or, we see them as strangers, out of our world, beyond our comprehension; and therefore well-nigh impossible to help, because we have not shared in their specific trouble or sin. For example, if we have not drunk excessively or at all, we look in wide-eyed amazement at the alcoholic who simply will not drop the bottle even when he or she sees the damage the bottle is causing.

We, being human, will distort our fellow men through our own spiritual eyes, unless and until we have the viewpoint of Christ. And we can only have this at last, by a complete and entire surrender of our selves (including our precious viewpoints) into the hands of the living God. Christ, alone, through His Holy Spirit, can give us the viewpoint which He has.

We believe the viewpoint of Christ must begin at the Cross of Christ. We cannot look at our fellow human beings with the viewpoint of Christ unless we can see them as He saw them – from the Cross. And the viewpoint of the Christ of the Cross is summed up in His own words spoken from that wrack of torture: "Father, *forgive* them, for they know not what they do."

The viewpoint of Christ, then, must be one of *no condemnation;* because a viewpoint of condemnation implies only one thing – self-righteousness within the heart of the one who condemns. And self-righteousness within the believer implies only one thing – the viewpoint of the *believer,* rather than the viewpoint of the One in whom he believes.

The circle is vicious and subtle.

But let us look at the pattern of the earthly life of our Lord for a moment. He was born in the lowest place a man can be born. I believe the Father picked out a stable for His Son's birthplace so no human being in all the ages after could say, "My background isn't good enough for me to become a Christian." No one . . . *no one* can be born in more meager surroundings than was our Lord.

From the point of view of His birth and the conditions surrounding it, can we condemn anyone among our fellow men no matter what their beginnings?

Or, let us look at the baptism of Jesus of Nazareth. "Then cometh Jesus from Galilee to Jordan unto John, to be baptized by him." To be baptized by John the Baptist, the people stood in line along the bank of the Jordan River. Can you picture Him, "The Lamb of God who taketh away the sin of the world," standing there patiently in line between a repentant thief and a woman of the streets, waiting His turn to be baptized with the others? We can picture Him doing nothing else. For He came to serve, not to be served. To save, not to condemn.

I testify from my own experience that if the one whom God used to lead me into a personal relationship with Jesus Christ had in any way, by the merest shadow of inference, chanced to condemn me during those first tense days as the Holy Spirit worked within my heart, I would not be writing these lines now. I know now how difficult it was for her. It is not easy for one who loves Jesus above all else to sit and hear His name blasphemed and used carelessly to punctuate casual conversation. It is not easy to have one's reason for living ridiculed. It is not easy to *be* ridiculed for Christ's sake.

But neither was it easy for Him to hang there hearing His own blood drain from His pain-twisted body and pray for the forgiveness of those who crucified Him. It did not take the usual dozen men to hold Jesus as they laid Him flat on the rude cross beam of the Cross. He lay there offering no resistance, making no move in self-defense as the blunt nails were driven into His outstretched hands and feet.

When the Cross was lifted up and dropped into the excavation in the ground, He made no cry of protest. He *prayed* for forgiveness for those who lifted Him up! *In this viewpoint of Christ from the Cross is the open secret of the victorious life of discipleship available to you and to me.*

If we are to have the viewpoint of Christ we cannot condemn, we can only *care.*

3.

No Hopeless Cases

When one true disciple of Jesus Christ thought on the vast, unending resources of the One whom he followed, he wrote: ". . . him that is able to do exceeding abundantly above all that we ask or think, according to the power that worketh in us."

The disciple, of course, was St. Paul. One who had, beyond the shadow of a doubt, the viewpoint of Jesus Christ. And, because he had this viewpoint, Paul knew for a fact that if *he* stayed sufficiently out of the way, the Holy Spirit of God could and would do *through* him (Paul) "exceeding abundantly above all that we ask or think."

Do we as followers of Jesus Christ really *believe* this? We say we believe the Bible to be the holy inspired Word of God. We say we believe the Pauline epistles, but do we actually believe that Jesus Christ *can* do exceedingly abundantly above all that we ask or think? If we do, then why don't we act like it by acting *on* that promise?

Do we or do we not believe that there are any *hopeless cases* where Jesus Christ is concerned? I am constrained to repeat that question – not for our sakes, but for His sake:

Do we or do we not believe that there are any hopeless cases where Jesus Christ is concerned?

What about the alcoholic or the inveterate liar or the gambler or the prostitute over whose darkened, frenzied, anxious lives have passed year after year of despair and failure? What about these people? As I write these lines I am half-listening for my telephone to ring, hoping against hope that a warm-hearted, gentle-mannered but seemingly hopeless alcoholic will call from somewhere in the cold, rainy shadows of this night along Chicago's Skid Row. I am trusting God that this boy will at last begin to *act* upon the knowledge he already possesses about his own "hopeless" case. This boy has known for ten years what he must do. He knows he must surrender one last thing to Christ. My friend and I have been praying and trying again with him for more than two years. His Christian mother in Little Rock, Arkansas, prays with us and believes with us that even though the years are piling up over her son's head, there is no such thing as a hopeless case with Jesus Christ.

There are no hopeless cases in Christ. If we believe there are, we are looking at the *sin* in the so-called hopeless case, or at the *sinner.* We simply are not looking at Christ and His resources. There are no hopeless cases with "him that is able to do exceeding abundantly above all that we ask or think."

A Christian believer shook my hand after a speaking engagement not long ago and wonderingly shook her head too as she asked: "How do you dare stand up there and promise that there are no hopeless cases when you've only been a Christian for such a short time? My brother-in-law's been a gambler for twenty years. We've never stopped praying that God would change him. But he's still at it. And we've just decided he's a hopeless case!"

I can stand anywhere and promise anyone that there are no hopeless cases in Christ on the full authority of the Son

Himself who said: "I am come that they might have life, and that they might have it more abundantly."

I can promise that in Him there are no hopeless cases because my Lord dared say of Himself what no mere human being ever dared say: "I am the way, the truth, and the life." And He did not mean a way of darkness and despair and sin and self-imprisonment. He meant the way of freedom and hope and eternal life. He meant the way *out* of darkness into the light of His love. And if Jesus Christ cannot back up the startling statements He made, if He cannot back up the claims He made, then He is the biggest phony who ever walked the face of this earth! If I cannot believe Him, whom can I believe?

More than that, even more than being able to put my whole weight down upon the promise of Christ, upon the spoken word of Christ, I can promise anyone, any time, anywhere that in Him are no hopeless cases because He was able to redeem *me!*

Quite quietly and quite calmly I stake my eternal life on the *fact* of my Saviour and my Lord, Jesus Christ. I know that when He looked down at me three and a half years ago, He did not see a hopeless case at all. He saw another creation of His, twisted all out of His plan and His nature by sin and self-will and hardness of heart. He saw one of His creations turned almost completely backwards to what He had intended her to be. But He did not see a hopeless case at all. Because He knew *Himself*. He saw *me* from the viewpoint of Himself. And He knew His own resources.

The true disciple *must* have the viewpoint of his Lord. And Jesus Christ knows that for Him, there are *no* hopeless cases.

4.

Innocence Is Not Purity

It may seem a presumptuous thing to do to begin a meditation by disagreeing point blank with Mr. Webster. And, I do not disagree in a general sense. But where two words in particular are concerned, I must disagree from the standpoint of their spiritual meaning to a true disciple of Christ.

Webster contends that they are practically synonymous. In two sections of his definition, he uses them interchangeably. Spiritually this is impossible. And yet many Christians not only use them interchangeably, to their own confusion of soul, but they also *act* upon them interchangeably, which results in the department of utter confusion for new Christians and non-believers.

What are these two words? They are: "innocence" and "purity."

Spiritually, I contend, they are not the same. And I have experienced in my own life, the confusion and heartache and inner damage which result from well-meaning Christians acting as though they *were* one and the same.

Isn't *innocence* the state in which babies are born? And

isn't *purity* an outright gift of God? Are we not *made pure*, because of what Jesus did for us on the Cross, only *after* we have been *born again* into that purity which comes from Him? And *only* from Him?

We are *born innocent* at our physical birth. But we are *made pure* by faith in Jesus Christ. And faith in Him means we dare to follow Him. "Surely he hath borne our griefs, and carried our sorrows: yet we did esteem him stricken, smitten of God, and afflicted. *But he was wounded for our transgressions,* he was bruised for our *iniquities;* the chastisement of our peace was upon him; and with his stripes we are healed. [Because] *all* we like sheep *have gone astray;* we have turned *every one to his own way;* and the Lord hath laid on *him* the iniquity of us *all.*"

"With *his* stripes we are healed" – *made pure.* We were *born* physically in *innocence.* We are *made pure* by Christ.

"Well," you say, "I believe all that. I do not contend that I was born pure. I am a true believer in the redemption of Jesus Christ. I know that includes me as just another sheep who went astray. I know I can claim no purity outside that which Christ has given me. I know I have been *made pure.*

All right, if we know that, then why is it that some of us do not behave as though we know it? Until she saw the true spiritual meanings of *purity* and *innocence* a well-meaning mother confused the issues in her family and in her own life by assuming that her innocence of certain sins of which her family was guilty somehow made *her* pure. She would shake her head prettily and say: "My goodness, I just don't see how they can drink that old stuff!" Or, "How can you swear every other breath like that?" Or "I never *wanted* to do those things!"

Sound familiar? Do you know someone like that? And does his very attitude seem to condemn you? Does this person's insistence that he has never even been tempted along *your* "disgusting lines" make you want either to bop him on his self-righteous head or run and hide your own head and give up trying to find Christ's answer to your own trouble? I know this is not a far-fetched reaction because I have had it myself. I have watched others smart under it. I have heard Christian young people sneer and act superior with their fellow students who drink. Thus they imply, if they do not say, "*I* just don't see *how* they can do it! *How* can they cheapen themselves?" The fellow students smart under their criticism and go on running from Christ.

Now, please do not misunderstand. Having lived in the world of paganism for almost eighteen years, I am the first to be glad and thankful when a Christian boy or girl grows all the way to maturity without sampling the world's interests. *But* I plead that they do just that – *grow all the way to maturity!* For Jesus' sake and for their own sakes. And for the sake of those whom they shut out of the kingdom by their own confusion of the spiritual meanings of the two words, "innocence" and "purity." I contend that innocence in an adult approaches stupidity. Again, do not misunderstand my meaning here. I do not advocate that anyone try the world in order to be delivered directly from worldly sins into the state of purity given only by Christ. He was without sin, and yet He reached down as far as is necessary to lift up the lowest sinner. He did not curl His lip and assume a lofty attitude and flaunt His innocence by reminding the populace that He "had never been interested in those things!"

I have tried my share and more of the pleasures of the world. And yet there are things I have never tried, simply because they did not interest me. But, do I have a right to curl my lip at those who *have* fallen on those points? Does my *innocence* of their particular sin give me a sense of purity on that point? If I think it does, God forgive me. I am not allowing Jesus Christ to live through me if this is so. Jesus was *pure* – not pompously innocent. And I am pure because He has *made* me pure.

Perhaps you have never loved the taste of whiskey. Perhaps you have never stolen anything. Perhaps you have never broken up a home. *But,* have you never shaded the truth in a conversation? Have you never told a white lie? Have you never lost your temper? Have you never criticized a fellow human being? Have you never been quick to fly to your own defense? Have you never been jealous? Have you never felt sorry for yourself? Are these not sins? Are they not transgressions for which He was wounded? Is anyone alive completely innocent of all these sins of the disposition? No. No one. But we can be made *pure,* thanks be to Him who "increased in wisdom and in stature"; who grew up into the maturity of deep sympathy and understanding of the failures of men; who not only expects us to do the same, but who daily offers us His grace and strength that we might be able to do it.

5.

His Purpose for Other People

In my own life, I have found that if I am truly following Christ, as a disciple follows his master, I do not have to concern myself about – myself. I do not have to wonder whether or not I will be at the right place at the right time in order to accomplish a certain end. I do not have to pick my friends. I do not need, even as a Christian, to hand out solutions to others in need. I do not need to do anything but obey the One whom I profess to trust enough to follow.

It is not easy for a convinced follower of Christ to keep silent many times when the answer to another's problem seems so evident. But there are times when the problems and sorrows of humanity are too terrible for words. And sympathetic silence, deep with the presence of Christ, performs its own miracles. We must be able to express our faith in words, but actions speak louder than words every time. We must not be disturbed if we do not always *have* the answer. But every minute of our lives we must *be* the answer.

We do not need to *have* the answer, but we do need to *be* the answer.

This is simply said, but not simply done. Coming completely into the viewpoint of Jesus Christ is painful, because it means the dying out of our points of view. But it also means the birth in us of *His* point of view, and that is added pain, since birth is usually more painful than death.

We must decide whether or not we are willing to "fill up that which is behind of the afflictions of Christ." Either we are willing or we are not willing. Only we can decide.

But if *you* decide within your own heart that you want to "walk in the light as he is in the light," in close discipleship with the Master, on an intimate, friendship basis, then there is still another aspect of His viewpoint which you must take for your own: *You must completely identify yourself with His purpose for other people.*

The real meaning of this is not apparent at first. At least the apparent meaning is far from the entire meaning. At first glance we would think this means that since He said, "Go ye into all the world and make disciples," our efforts toward bringing others into the Christian life would constitute "identifying ourselves with His purpose for other people."

This is true. But it is only part of the deepest meaning of complete identification with His intent in the individual lives of those with whom we come in contact. We simply cannot help winning *some* if we ourselves are in complete contact with Christ. We cannot be in contact with Him, unless He indwells us and lives again on this earth in our bodies. And since He Himself said: "I, if I be lifted up . . . will draw all men unto me," we will, if His words are true, win *some*. Those of us who love Him and rejoice in the fulness of the wonder of the life hid with Christ in God find it difficult to keep still about this enchanted life. We don't witness because we believe it is expected of us. We simply do it because we can't help it. And so, winning others, as essential as it is, comes as a fruit of belonging entirely. And we, who mean to go all the way with Him, must delve deeper and find still other ways of identifying ourselves with His purpose in our lives.

In my experience with this deeper delving, I have stumbled and blundered most noticeably at the times when I felt perfectly justified in using my *common sense.* I do not believe we can repeat too often the dust-raising truth that *if common sense had been enough, Jesus Christ would not have needed to die!*

Let me illustrate by a personal experience. Sometime ago after a broadcast I was asked to talk to a brilliant actor, who had struggled vainly with the bottle for years. Now, normally the opportunity to talk with anyone from my old world B.C. is one of the dear delights of my heart, but this particular request seemed to offer a few serious complications. I hesitated because a travel schedule had given me only four hours sleep the night before, the broadcast was an unusually difficult one to direct, *and* I was scheduled to leave town a bit after dawn the next morning for three speaking engagements in two different cities in one day.

I have long since learned that mere physical fatigue need not stop Christ's work for long. If we stay attached to the *vine,* we are constantly in line to receive the *continuous* flow of living water. And so, trying His strength has turned into an exciting experience. I was not worried about *feeling* tired. But I did hesitate momentarily for this reason: What about the three congregations of people waiting to hear me the next day? Was I being fair to drag in a tired, limp excuse for a speaker when so *many* people were involved? Common sense would have said: "Consider the previously made engagements. This actor lives in Chicago. You can talk to him when you come back. You know it will be well after midnight before you get to bed if you get involved in a conversation of that type."

Common sense said that. But I asked Jesus what His purpose in this actor's life was – for that night. I got no answer at once. But after about ten minutes in the silence with the One in whose will I want to live every minute, I had my answer. And after our conversation that night, driving home alone, my friend, the actor, stopped his car, put his head down on the steering wheel and received Jesus as his Saviour and his Lord. Having been very much aware of Christ's complete mastership of my every action and thought that night, I had talked at length about that aspect of the Christian life. So when my friend stepped "in," he knew it meant turning his back on himself – *completely.* The fact that Jesus *mastered* me intrigued him. He came in *all* the way. Jesus does not always figure in numbers. And we cannot "figure" His purpose from our viewpoint. We must do our looking and our acting – *every* minute of every hour of every day – from the viewpoint of Christ.

6.

Self-realization vs. Self-expenditure (I)

THERE IS SOMETHING definitely attractive in the schools of "new thought" and the cults of self-development. Much of their positive thinking could make more victorious Christians of the true followers of the divine Son of God, Jesus of Nazareth, whom the cultists merely admire as a great man. After all, Jesus Himself said, "*Let* not your heart be troubled." That requires some positive affirming on our part. (However, it is a mystery to me how an unregenerate person, a mere imitator of Christ, *could* simply ignore the pieces and let not his heart be troubled if that heart found itself in a shattered state.) There is something attractive about the self-development cults. In fact, it is so attractive that they are drawing off bored, tired, nominal Christians into their ranks every day.

And what is this attraction? The bane of the Christian's existence! *Self.* But to the man outside of Christ, the most important person in the world is *himself.* And when a religion (such as Hinduism) or a new thought school (such as the various scientific pseudo-Christian movements) encourages a man to "bring out the best within" and "develop" that all important person – himself, naturally he is going to summon his fellow man and follow after the group that tells him he's going to be just fine when he gets the best in him all shined up and declared righteous by – himself.

I repeat that reborn Christians could take some pointers here. Once we have dumped our own sinful selves into the hands of Jesus Christ our Redeemer, *then* we can expect the very best from those redeemed selves. If we cannot, in fact, if we *do* not, we underestimate our Redeemer. I believe that a "new creature," by the power of the indwelling Holy Spirit, *can* "let not" his heart be troubled. He is *enabled* to do it. He is not doing it under his own human steam; he is *enabled* to do it by Christ's indwelling presence.

None of this is new to the thoughtful disciple of Christ. But it is needed to preface what we must consider together now, as we move toward the end of our thinking on some of the characteristics of the true disciple of Jesus Christ. Here is the focal point: We must shift our perspective from *self-realization* to *self-expenditure.*

If we are to be disciples, we must have the viewpoint of Christ, and in order to have His viewpoint, we must stop trying to *realize* our *selves*, and begin *spending ourselves* for Him. Back in my B.C. days, I was an accomplished spendthrift. Now, the Lord has taken that sin, turned it inside out, redeemed it, but is still *fulfilling* that desire to spend by allowing me the unspeakable joy and stimulus of *spending myself for Him.* I have found Jesus Christ to be the kind of God who never asks us to give up a single thing which He does not replace with "good measure pressed down . . . and running over." When my dear friend, Ellen, led me into the presence of the One who transformed my life, she needed at the last moment to urge me only to this extent: "Give Him all of your life, and He will hurl all of His life back into its place."

Could I resist an exchange like that? No, I could not.

Thank God, I did not. And although the deep-down excitement that flooded my very being that day, October 2, 1949, when this eternal transaction was made, has ebbed and flowed at times, not once have I lost sight of the fact that in the terms of that eternal transaction, *I* had promised to give Him *all of my* life. I became aware also that the transaction was continuous as well as instantaneous. As with all of us, at times I have jerked myself back from His hands, and have started "throwing cues" according to what I considered good timing. But at no time in my entire life have I known heart misery to equal my own when I have done this – even for a few minutes. And so, my soul vibrates with joy that I have been made aware that if I continue to give to Him, He continues to give to me – good measure, pressed down, and shaken together, and running over.

And when I speak of spending myself, I do not mean the long tiring trips and loss of sleep entailed by a top-heavy speaking schedule. I do not mean the nights spent in pounding the typewriter in order to meet script and book deadlines. These could easily fall into the category of *self-realization* – *if* my conception of self-expenditure ended there.

But, as a disciple of Jesus Christ, I believe that we have no right to be anything but doormats to every human being who does not know the *full measure* of joy we know in belonging to Jesus personally. And the statement should be examined closely, because it implies much more than it states. Every human being who does not know the full measure of joy might seem to mean every *non-believer.* But it means much more than that. I feel ashamed if for His sake, I am at times unwilling to be or careless about being "broken bread and poured out wine" for all Christians who have *not* found the *fullness* of the life hid with Christ in God. I have wept into my pillow many nights because of the multitudes of unhappy, unvictorious, worried, anxious Christians with whom I have spoken here and there. And because I have finally yielded my own stubborn (converted) self into the hands of Him who surrendered His life for *me,* I can only be "broken bread and poured out wine" until these anxious Christians as well as the non-believers with whom I come in contact are brought into the fullness of the life hid with Christ in God.

If we are trying to realize the best in ourselves and save our energies for our own troubles, we do not have the viewpoint of Jesus Christ. We are *saving* ourselves in the face of what He did to save us *from* ourselves. We are saving ourselves when, for love of Him, we should be *spending* ourselves.

7.

Self-realization vs. Self-expenditure (II)

(I COULD FILL THE PAGES of an entire book with what I have discovered about the miracles that result in a redeemed human life when the will is fully surrendered to Jesus Christ. A fully surrendered will and a completely yielded life mean a life of true discipleship, with fruit hanging from every thriving branch. Christ allows the fruit to grow on the branches while He, the Vine, quietly and lovingly supports and feeds each branch with His own life).

We continue thinking together in this *essential* characteristic of the true disciple: *self-expenditure* in place of self-realization.

We resign as masters of the universe and allow Christ to take over at conversion. But, just as the same basic law of nature that brings the bud to the apple tree for the first time continues operative between the Creator and the apple tree for the duration of the tree's life, so the same divine law that brings about our spiritual rebirth remains operative between the disciple and the Creator forever.

In the deepest sense, perhaps we could say He *creates*

discipleship in us. Our part is to let Him do it. No human being alive *prefers* in his own raw, human nature, to deny himself for others. No human being *prefers* to lose his life in order to save it. He prefers to save his life and take his chances on finding still more. This is not observation culled from tomes on the psychology of human nature. This is fact from my own life B.C. Until Jesus Christ reached down and took me to Himself, my philosophy of life (if such I had in fact) ran something like this: "Get all I can get for myself today and then take my chances on being able to get even more tomorrow!"

This did not make me an unpleasant, greedy creature. This simply made me resemble people. I was generous and kind to those about whom I cared, or who pleased me for one reason or another; but I would not give one iota of myself for someone about whom I did not care. I was the most important person in the world to me. Period.

I probably would not have admitted it then, because indeed, in all honesty, I simply did not see myself that way. How could I? That is looking at human nature through the clear eyes of Christ. He sees anything that comes between Himself and His creatures for whom He died, as sin. And the self in that creation is the root of *all* that comes between. My overdose of self blinded me *to* myself.

With these stinging truths in mind, examine your Christian life with me — right now, as I examine mine under the light of Him who *is* light. Is your cup running over? Is mine? If they are not, they should be. Jesus has plenty of living water, and if our cups are only half full it must mean they are simply not clean enough for Him to fill. He will not, He *cannot* pour His living water into a dirty cup.

Now, we can soil our cups and pitchers in many ways. Worry, fear, anxiety, stubbornness, jealousy, bitterness, resentment, temper, a critical nature, a sharp tongue – any or all of these and more can so smudge our lives that the living water, because of God's own holy nature, cannot be poured into them.

But the most frequent cause of smudge among Christians which I have found is this: *The seemingly unthinking way in which we continue to live our own lives.* When I say "unthinking," I mean that it is almost as though many are innocent of the fact that they are continuing to live their own lives. We attend our churches, work among the church groups, serve on committees, teach classes, tithe, give religious books to non-believers, intercede in prayer, keep our moral lives above reproach – and yet, we are living self-lives. Our families and our homes and our offices and our church *activities* are in the center of our lives. All for the glory of God, of course, we strive to do a better job than the other fellow did. Our churches are filled with well-meaning, hard-working, respectable Christian men and women who have their Christian *selves* in the center of their lives and *not* the person of Jesus Christ.

Jesus Christ's *person* was magnetic and powerful enough literally to *pull* me out of a life of paganism and draw me to Himself. Perhaps it is *simpler* (not easier, but *simpler*) for me to keep Him in the center of my life. After having steamed through thirty-three years under a full head of self-realization, I can do nothing now but shift completely to the viewpoint of the One who gentled my striving sinful spirit and restored me to the freedom and fulfillment He meant me to have "in the beginning."

You may spend more nights a week on church work than you spend with your family. But what would be your reaction if an alcoholic called you on the telephone at 3:30 A.M. and began mumbling and mouthing at you about the tough way life treats him? I may write half the night and speak four times the next day, but how much of the spirit of Christ will I show when, at the close of the last speaking date that next day (when my eye-lids are being propped open by the grace of God), some well-rested Christian brother comes up to me and says, "I'm glad God is no respecter of persons and that he saved you, Miss Price, but I'm sorry you had to sink so low first. And another thing, Miss Price, on your radio program seven weeks ago you said that 'whosoever believeth *in* him should not perish,' and it should have been 'whosoever believeth *on* him!'" Will I smile at that well-meaning brother and offer him my hand, mindful of the nail prints in the hand of the One who *was* no respecter of persons (thank God!) when He did reach down to save me? Will I view life from the perspective of my own touchy self, or have I truly shifted my perspective from self-realization, from self-protection, to self-*expenditure?*

What of the Christians who have never invited a non-believer to their homes for dinner? Who refuse to entertain a new, stumbling Christian because that new Christian still smokes or drinks? Who keep themselves so busy with breaking fancy cakes and pouring countless cups of coffee for the sake of "Christian fellowship" that they have no time left to be "broken bread and poured out wine" for the sake of bringing some desperate man or woman into the fellowship of Christ?

We cannot condemn our Christian brothers when we face these facts. I must confess I did at first, so stunned was I to see how complacently the average Christian moves through his respectable and protected life, literally ignoring those outside the walls of his own particular doctrinal belief. Having been "out there" and left alone by Christians for so long, my heart broke for Jesus' sake; and at first I condemned in my heart. Now, my heart still breaks for Jesus' sake, but my condemnation has turned, by His grace, to intercession for those comfortable Christian brothers and sisters who have not found the fullness and the joy of complete self-*expenditure* for the One who "is not willing that *any* should perish."

Discoveries

Concerning My Reason for Living

8.

To Me to Live Is Not to Be Religious

Opening another line of discovery together, let us ask ourselves this question: Can I honestly and without reservation say, "To me to live is *Christ*"?

As disciples, *if* we are true disciples, this must be entirely a reality with us. And since we can delude ourselves and fool our friends quite innocently on this point, I feel we must give it careful scrutiny. Just what exactly does it mean? What does it mean to you when you read or repeat, "To me to live is Christ"? What does it *do* to you? Does it ring any bells? Does it cause your heart to race with joy? Does it make you want to look up, just for the sake of knowing that you can look up and see no shadow between you and this Christ?

Or is it just another Scripture text?

If it is that, repeating the words or reading them from the Bible will do no more than stir up that respect which we hold for the written-down revelation of God which we have between the covers of the greatest Book.

Or, perhaps it arouses no more than admiration within

you for the childlike humility of St. Paul, who allowed himself to be changed from a Christ-hater to one who could say without reservation that for him to live was Christ.

This altogether startling phrase could and does bring about many reactions ranging from utter perplexity in the non-believer to the quiet ecstacy of the saint whose lips form the words with the joy and certainty that add up to "foolishness to the natural man."

We pass by these varied reactions now, however, to look at the ways in which sincere, well-meaning, devoted Christians can *un*consciously misinterpret it or rephrase it. Saint Paul said: "To me to live is Christ." But how easy is it for us to say: "To me to live is to be *religious!*"

Does *this* interpretation of the immortal words ring any bells with you? With me, I am afraid if it rang anything it would be a buzzer. I do not even like the sound of the word "religious." I like it even less than I did before I surrendered my life to Christ. There are many religions. Basically they are all attempts to bridge the gap between God and man. But in only one of them, the Gospel of Christ, does God reach down for man. In the others, man reaches vainly, pathetically, anxiously toward God. And so to me, living the Christian life is not "being religious," it is belonging to a *Person* who has reached down for me. And yet, according to the lack of vitality, the lack of dynamic, the frigidity of many so-called Christian lives, this text *must* be one of the most misinterpreted texts in the entire Bible. If I say, "To me to live is to be religious," I am missing the mark entirely.

I am not only missing the mark the Lord expects me to hit, I am putting emphasis entirely in the wrong place. For example, if we say, "To me to live is to be religious," how quickly we can tread respectably and stiffly into formalism. If we say, "To me to live is to be religious," how swiftly we will mount our pedestals and attempt to serve those beneath us, without once bending our necks to look at their agony of soul and mind and body. If we say, "To me to live is to be religious," how *unlike* our Lord we will become.

For can we be like Him if we are garbed in our religious regalia high atop our pious pedestals? From that vantage point can we show the world the brotherly love of the One who stood in line with sinners to wait His turn to be baptized? Can we show the world the gentle heart of the One who always took time to heal a blind beggar and take notice of a widow's mite? Can we show the world the almighty meekness of the One who turned His blood-filled eyes to the Father to ask forgiveness for those who caused Him to shed that blood drop by precious drop? Can we, sitting on our religious pedestals, convince the world that *we* know He hung there for our sakes too? Can we show forth from a pedestal the nature of the One who was born so low no sinner could possibly claim a more lowly beginning? Can we sit on a religious pinnacle and convince anyone that we follow a Lord who was purposely born in a stable? Can we proclaim from atop our pious perches that we *serve* the One who *wants* to wash the feet of the world *through* us?

After having lived in darkness, I am much aware of the freedom and satisfaction of having the world know there is no stain or shadow in my life now; that I am forgiven by and restored to my Father. But if I say, "To me to live is to be religious or respectable or respected," I am putting the blessings of my new life in the center and not the Blesser. If I am impressed with my new purity, can I expect Jesus to be able to reach down *through* me and lift up a bitter atheist who quite naturally hates my purity? Only when I see my own holiness as His holiness poured *into* my life, only when I see my adequate life as a result of having emptied my life of my *self* and of having that empty space filled with His victorious Spirit, then and only then can His love flow through me to those in need, to those whom He needs as they need Him. To me to live is *not* to be religious. To me to live is – Christ.

Is it true with you? It can be before you turn this page.

9.

To Me to Live Is Not to Serve Humanity

THERE ARE MANY, too many words which are consciously or unconsciously substituted for the name of Christ in the penetrating phrase of Paul: "To me to live is Christ."

We have already looked at some length into the dangers of living as though the phrase read, "To me to live is to be *religious.*" Now let us face another substitution which is so often made in this verse in place of His wonderful name. Do not many thousands of well-meaning Christians revise the phrase to read this way: "To me to live is to serve *humanity*"?

Now, on this point, I want to be clearly understood. As a new Christian, I am daily surprised and sometimes shocked at the seeming indifference to the sufferings of humanity shown by many of those who make the most effusive Christian professions. Jesus did not say we had to believe in His atonement; He simply died and made it a reality for us when we take it by faith. He did not demand that we believe in His resurrection; He simply — arose! He does not demand that we believe in His coming again; He will simply return one day in His time. In fact, Jesus did not demand that we believe very many things on a list. But He did command that we love one another. He asked us to love God with our whole being and to love our neighbors as we love ourselves.

If we remember that on our own we are the most important persons in the world to ourselves, that last is quite an order. Literally, of course, it does not only mean the person who lives next door or even in our neighborhood. It means every human being on earth. I do not believe it means that we can respond emotionally in a positive way to every creature, but it surely does mean that we must be as *concerned* for the welfare of others as we are for ourselves. And *that* is a big order. Do we fly to the defense of others as quickly as we fly to the defense of ourselves?

No comment.

Do we pity members of the church down the street or of the opposition political party when failure strikes them as we pity our precious selves?

No comment.

Why? Because we do not love and want to serve our fellow man as we love and want to serve ourselves or those to whom we happen to react favorably.

Daily I have to spend time before the humble Christ, who asked me to love *everyone,* to allow Him to touch and transform the tender, sore spots of self-esteem and snobbery still showing up in me. It hurts to have them touched. It makes me reel and tremble for the moment to see Him changing – actually changing one of my old precious opinions of a certain person into His opinion of that person. It knocks crutch after crutch out from under my swaying ego. But when the operation is done, how relieved I am not to have to be upset or irritated the next time that particular kind of person enters my life. How safe I feel then not to need that crutch any longer to prop up my self-esteem.

Much of the barb throwing, however, between the conservatives and the liberals of Christendom, has resulted from this very point of serving humanity. The liberals tend to rephrase Paul this way: "To me to live is to serve humanity!" One such liberal friend of mine made a pithy statement to me not long ago. She contends that the liberals need to love the Lord more and the fundamentalists need to love the people more. I agree.

A social gospel alone, where the needs of humanity are placed uppermost, is but a half-gospel. But those of us who believe in a complete Gospel *must,* for the sake of Christ, learn to love the *whole man – not just his soul.* Just as we must also want to *save his soul* and not merely his body and his mind.

It is easy, exceedingly easy, to become eccentric in our sincere efforts to be true disciples of Christ. And if the emphasis is put upon any one corner of the life, it tips. So, just as "To me to live is to be religious" is off center, so is "To me to live is to serve humanity" off-center. *Ec*centric.

Thousands upon thousands of men and women all over the world spend their lives pouring themselves out for humanity. This is the highest human level of life. Truly, no one could deny that this is the highest *natural* life. But, the true disciple of the divine Jesus Christ, God incarnate, does not need to be tied to the earth by even this highest *human* or *natural* achievement. Only the twice-born Christian has access to the *super*-human and the *super*-natural, by the power of the indwelling Holy Spirit. We are insured against heart-break this way. Since the Person of the Holy Spirit is one with God the Father and with Jesus Christ, He will not "let Himself down" as He lives His life through us. Humanity will turn its back on a man. Divinity through Jesus Christ will turn the man into His own image. Humanity will break a man's heart; divinity, through Jesus Christ, will *mend* that heart.

Serving humanity is a noble aim. But it is only one of the inevitable fruits of the life of the man or woman whose every thought and word and deed shout to the world:
"To me to live is Christ!"

10.

To Me to Live Is Not to Serve Christ

We will speak elsewhere in this book about the startling fact (to some) that Jesus Christ does not want our *talents*, He wants *us*. Of course, He wants our talents too, but not *without all* the rest of us thrown in. With this in mind, and with our minds wide open, let us look still more deeply into a popular rephrasing of the all-inclusive statement of St. Paul: "To me to live is Christ."

We have thought together so far upon these rephrasings of Paul's profound declaration: "To me to live is to be *religious*"; then, "To me to live is to serve *humanity*." Now we go even deeper than these two convenient interpretations. We look honestly at an interpretation of the immortal words which would at first glance seem to be synonymous with what Paul was actually saying. Consider this with me: "To me to live is to *serve* Christ."

"To me to live is to serve Christ." "To me to live is Christ." Did not this Christ say, "Go ye into all the world and make disciples"? Did not this same Christ say, "The fields are white to harvest"? Yes, He did. And so, we must lift many of the top layers off the familiar testimony of Paul in order to reach the place at the heart of his statement which shows us the grave difference between a simple *belonging* to Christ and merely *serving* Him.

For reasons known only to Him, the Master put me almost immediately into the thick of the harvest field. One year and one week after my conversion to Jesus Christ, I stood in the control room of a large radio station directing the only "big time" Christian dramatic program about lives which had been transformed as mine had been transformed by the touch of the Holy Spirit of God. The program was well named – "Unshackled." Every fiber of its writer-producer's being vibrated with the consciousness that she, too, had been "unshackled," just as surely and from just as defeated a life as any man or woman who reached the black alleys and the dusty gutters of Chicago's Skid Row. The mail count climbed, the studio audience increased, magazine writers began to call for interviews and the requests for speaking dates poured in – more each month, until there were not enough days in the week to fill them and still continue writing "Unshackled." People clasped my hand and from sincere hearts said: "Oh, how wonderfully the Lord is using you! How glorious is your great *service* for Christ!"

And my eyes filled with tears of wonder along with theirs as I moved through the glowing days with the amazement of a child suddenly set down in a toy shop a hundred miles square. Offers came for more radio programs, for T.V. programs, for magazine articles, for columns. And instead of feeding my previously over-sized vanity, by His grace the opposite took place. I began to understand what Paul meant when he said: "I determined not to know anything among you, save Jesus Christ, and him crucified."

The Crucified Himself overshadowed me *and* my new Christian service. I became more and more drawn toward the pursuit of a deeper personal walk with Christ, my new Lord. I was grateful for the confidence of God's people who urged me into wider and wider fields of service, and I recognized the need for it. Daily, I became more and more aware of how *much* Jesus needed disciples in whose very bodies He could walk the earth once more, ministering to His lost sheep. After having been one of those lost sheep for thirty-three years, my arms ached to take every troubled human being in the world to my heart, where I knew they would at least be close to Him who held my heart forever.

And yet, above the din of the world's need, above the definite call into a life of service, I heard the unmistakable high, clear notes of the call of His heart to mine: "Come unto *me* . . . Learn of *me* . . . Learn of *me!*"

I answered His call to my heart. In just three short years, I am learning to walk with Jesus, as the disciples walked with Him down the dusty roads two thousand years ago. This is no accomplishment of mine other than my willingness to seek *Him* before I sought greater fields of His service. It is a warm and wonderful feeling to share the fellowship of the blessed community as one after another of God's people clasp my hand in love and encouragement, but following Him into the deeper life means less of this and more hours of silence and weeping and crying out for mercy as one after another of my pet opinions and prejudices and abilities are cut into and changed and reshaped according to His intention. It is far easier to serve than to be changed. It is easier to speak from a platform than to be spoken to in the silence by the One who sees my heart laid bare. It is easier to write and direct an exciting dramatic radio program than it is to spend the cold morning hours on my knees being redirected by Him who alone knows His purpose for my life. But when I am altogether His, and walking minute by minute in His strength, He can automatically use me more because then and only then can He serve others through me. As long as I'm there, He can't get through, can He?

No, and if you have not discovered this in your own life, I beg of you to discover it now in the silence with Him, so that you too may say, "To me to live is not to *serve* Christ; to me to live *is* Christ!"

11.

To Me to Live Is Not to Be Christlike

IN DIGGING into the depths of the meaning of Saint Paul's glowing testimony, "To me to live is Christ," we should seem to be able to come up with a conclusion right now and then move on to another thought. We should be able to tie it all up this way: if we say, "To me to live is *to be* or *to do* – *anything*," we are on the wrong track. The little infinitives should give us the key. And indeed in a general sense, they do. The very implication of the "to be" or "to do" shifts *us* into the place where, according to Paul, *Christ* must be.

And yet, there is one more "to be" which is so often used innocently when one is trying to let his or her life say, "To me to live is Christ," that I feel we must dig into this one before we move on. What is it? Just this: "To me to live is to be *Christlike!*"

Have you ever tripped over this one? I have many times. Those of you who, along with me, have been brought into a close, personal relationship with Christ out of another world, may have tripped over this rephrasing of Paul's famous line even more than those who have lived merely respectable Christian lives. Nevertheless, I feel quite sure that if we face facts honestly, we can all say that at one time or another in our Christian lives we have been absorbed with our own holiness. Or, we have become so preoccupied with checking up on our own spiritual growth that we have neglected or have completely forgotten that the Lord God said, "Feed my sheep" as well as "Be ye holy." We can become so taken up with wishful thinking concerning our own spiritual growth that without realizing it *we* are again in the center of our own lives and Christ and His purpose have been moved to the margins.

It is well to remember the familiar story about the little girl who kept digging up the seed she had planted to see whether or not it was growing. Disciples of Jesus Christ who become fascinated with their own potential resemblance to their Master slip dangerously near the brink of the so-called "new thought" cults. Absorption with our own holiness or our spiritual progress is *self*-development, isn't it? If Jesus did a finished work on the Cross, do we need to do more than stay in position to have His great redemption become a completed reality in our lives?

Please do not misunderstand me. I do not mean to imply that we must not "walk in the light as he is in the light," that we must not keep constant vigil over our relationship with Christ. I merely mean that those well-intentioned men and women who become impressed with their own growing resemblance to Christ *or* depressed by their growing lack of it are quite likely to put a sudden stop to the entire procedure. The living water will sink to a low level and stagnate. And we will wonder why when we have been giving such implicit attention to our own spiritual growth.

Did not our Master say we could not add one inch to our height by any effort of our own? Did He not say that He is the Vine and we are the branches? And did you ever hear of a branch clenching its leaves together in verdant agony as it pleaded with the vine to send down more sap? No.

The branch merely stays fastened on to the vine, and *expects* the supply of life-giving sap sufficient for its growth. The lilies and the tall green corn of the fields just stay in position to receive the sunlight and the rain and the nutriment from the soil.

Dr. Anna Mow (happily for me, my friend) gives this formula for one of those knotty, black days when we are inclined to put our spiritual conditions in the center of our attention. First of all, Anna checks whether or not she has had enough sleep the night before. If she has had, she checks the possibility that she has hurt someone inadvertently or intentionally. If this is not true, then she goes over the resentment and bitterness and self-pity departments. If all is well there and she can simply find no reason for her spiritual indigestion, she throws back her head and laughs her contagious, characteristic laugh and says: "All right, *you* stay here, Anna Mow, I'm going on with the Lord!" I've tried it too. It works.

God did say, "Be ye holy as I am holy"; but no amount of fascination with our holiness or lack of it will *increase* our holiness. He tells us to be holy, but then He sets about making us that way *when* we yield ourselves utterly into His lovely hands.

My dear friend and companion, Ellen Riley, twinkles with good-humored laughter at herself when she tells of her first years as a Christian. She was organist at the Methodist church back in our home town of Charleston, West Virginia. And so fascinated was she with the change in her personality after her conversion to Christ that she used to sneak long, admiring glances at herself in the mirror above the console of the big pipe organ on a Sunday morning as she sighed inwardly and thought: *Oh, isn't it wonderful? I'm growing more spiritual looking every day I live!*

This story always brings a relieved laugh from any group of Christians, because we are all guilty of becoming preoccupied in greater or lesser degrees with our own purity. And any movement of our *full* attention away from the face of Christ toward even our own Christlikeness is a dangerous and a confusing thing. It is risky for us and confusing for those who depend upon us. As glorious as holiness is when we see it actually happening in our own lives, we must not say, "To me to live is to be Christlike"; we must say and mean and then our very lives will proclaim "To me to live *is* Christ!"

12.

To Me to Live Is Christ

We have seen that it is an easy procedure for a well-meaning follower of Jesus Christ innocently to rephrase the singing words of Saint Paul: "To me to live is Christ." We have seen how easy it is to say, "To me to live is to be religious, to serve humanity, to serve Chirst, to be Christlike." We have also seen that any of these variations will result in sub-Christianity and an unvictorious life. Why? Because to a true disciple of Christ, his life is not a religion; it is the simple following of a living Person. And to him, this immortal testimony comes as naturally as breathing:

"To me to live is – Christ!"

So far as I know, I can claim this testimony as my own. *To me to live is the person of Jesus Christ.* And this is true for many reasons. Among them: I was not led into a *way of life* when I received Jesus Christ as my own personal Saviour and Lord and Master. I have dedicated this little book to the disciple of Christ who led me so carefully and so lovingly, *not* into a "better way of life," but into a close, intimate walk with the *person* of my new Lord.

I never think on the fact that I have found a better way

to live on this earth. But I think often and joyfully about the living Person who so recently drew me unto Himself — forever. I don't think, "Now, I can stay out of trouble"; but I live by the very fact of the Person who overcame my trouble on the Cross. I don't think, "Now, God will comfort me when tragedy strikes my life"; but I do rest in the tremendous knowledge that should tragedy strike, the person of the Holy Spirit will be right there to show me how to *use* that tragedy for His glory. I don't think, "Now that I'm a Christian, I won't drink anymore, or throw my money to the four winds and wind up deeper and deeper in debt." This is all true, but I don't dwell on that negative aspect of the whole thing. Instead, I just let the involuntary smile play away at the corners of my mouth because now that I belong to Jesus and He belongs to me, I don't *need* to drink. And I've *found* the fulfillment and excitement in Him, on which I used to have to spend my money. I don't think, "Now that I'm a Christian I must tithe and live conservatively"; I just return every dollar to Him at the outset and let Him spend it for me. "To me to live is Christ" because I was led, not into a better way of life, but into an intimate minute by minute walk with a living Person.

I have dedicated this book of discoveries to the one who convinced me *not* merely of a "plan of salvation" (I wouldn't have understood that phrase at all), but who *introduced* me *personally* to the Saviour, who did His own convincing in my heart and mind. As beautiful and as awe-inspiring as is the divine plan of God for the salvation of His lost sheep, it has little or no meaning for the pagan mind. Mine was a completely pagan mind, believing in nothing higher than my own wits. And so, the most careful intellectual or Scriptural explanation of the plan of salvation would have confused me; and since my pride would not allow me to admit confusion of any sort, any theological explanation of salvation would have only served to slam the door of the kingdom in my face.

But, thanks be to Christ, He had convinced my friend of His own *personal wonder.* He had drawn her to Himself out of a time of heartbreak and personal tragedy. She had found Him to be the living God with healing in His hands. She loved Him with all her heart when she met me, and she merely stood aside and let Him woo me unto Himself. "To me to live is Christ," because I was not merely intellectually convinced of a divine plan for the salvation of my eternal soul. I was permitted to fall in love with the Lover of my soul, Jesus Christ, the *living* Son of God.

This little book is dedicated to the disciple of Jesus Christ, who through her consecrated life allowed Him to confront me face to face with Himself. She did not attempt to frighten me into the kingdom by threatening me with an almost superstitious wielding of the written-down revelation of God, the Holy Bible. She knew I did not believe the Bible at all. And if she had had *only* Scripture texts (as dynamic as they are to me now) *then,* she would have been fighting a losing battle. She won me to Christ though, because she allowed the Holy Spirit full rein in *her* mind and imagination, and therefore guaranteed no blunders in timing. I was led gently and completely into a new life with Jesus Christ in a hotel room, and there was no one present with me but my friend, Ellen, and Jesus Christ.

After He had transformed me, then my desire for the wonder of the Holy Scriptures leaped into being; but if for some fantastic reason I should be told that the New Testament is all a mistake, I would still go right on following my living Lord. After all, the early Christians in the upper room had only the Holy Spirit Himself. If some reader decides from this paragraph that I do not believe with all my heart in the inspired Word of God as we have it in the Bible, I beg him to reread this meditation again more thoughtfully.

But to me to live is not the Bible, because the Word became flesh, not printer's ink; and as glorious as is that Spirit-inspired account of God's divine nature and plan, its light is to me the *person* of my Lord, Jesus Christ. Without reservation, "To me to *live is Christ.*"

And this same Christ, available to me personally through His Holy Spirit, has proved Himself to me; so that I am not only a converted Christian, I am a totally *convinced* Christian, "strengthened with might by His Spirit in the inner man." Jesus Christ, the Holy Spirit and the Father have at last become One to me. And so, more than ever now, "To me to live is Christ," because all I need know of the Father is what He showed me in His Son.

Discoveries

Concerning a Number of Wonder-filled Things

13.

Are You Free?

ARE YOU FREE? I know you live in a free country, but are you really *free?* I have lived in a free country since my first birth on June 22, 1916, but I have only been *free* since my second birth, October 2, 1949, when I was invaded from above and set free of my *self* by the transforming touch of the Holy Spirit.

This startling fact is almost humorous when I confess that most of those thirty-three years which passed between my first birth and my second birth were spent in loud protest against any kind of restraint and even louder declarations of personal freedom. I had to be free! I wanted everyone to leave me alone to live my own life as I wanted to live it – in freedom. I was a rebel from the word "go." I hated confinement and convention. I detested being disciplined. In fact to me "discipline" was the most unpleasant word outside of "obedience" in the entire English language, until I was thirty-three years old. Although my years numbered thirty-three, I had stopped growing emotionally at about a precocious sixteen. In my thirties, at the head of my own business, I was still asserting myself like an adolescent, kicking and yelling at life: "Leave me alone . . . I'm the type who just *has* to be free!" All this is too sadly true of some Christians who demand to remain the type that insists, "This is the way I am!" *Can't Jesus Christ change our natures?*

But back to freedom. In spite of the kicking and yelling for freedom all my thirty-three years, only *now* that I am at last free of my *self*, am I truly *free.* And, hold on to your hats, I found this freedom through *obedience* and *discipline!*

If we examine the inorganic matter in the bottom of a pool, we find it to be trapped there as dead matter. But, when that dead, inorganic matter is invaded from above by the root of a water lily, drawn up and *confined* within the disciplinary process of giving of itself to the lily, then and only then is that once-dead matter *free* to grow. Indeed, for the first time it is free to – live.

Not until I was invaded from above by the Holy Spirit was I free to live. "He that hath the Son hath life; and he that hath not the Son of God hath not life." Now, *drawn up* into the life of the Lily of the Valley, I am free to give of my once-dead self as nourishment to others. *Confined* in the glorious disciplinary process of giving of myself to Jesus Christ and His sheep, I am, for the very first time, free to grow.

Take the train off its track, and how far does it advance toward its destination? Suppose the engineer decides to indulge a sudden whim of his own and make the run between Chicago and Denver without a track to confine him. Will his passengers ever reach Denver?

Only in complete holy obedience to the merest whisper of Jesus Christ do we truly find the freedom for which we were created. And I firmly believe He created that desire for freedom within us all. The Father's heart grieves when His creatures are chained to earthly habits and beliefs. He created us to be free. And in Himself, through Christ, He provides that freedom.

A missionary friend of mine, a truly radiant Christian, once told me my life now reminded him of a flight he took over India some years ago. He smiled as he recalled the trip. It seems the pilot asked my friend if he would like to fly the plane, assuring him that if he did just as the pilot instructed, all would be well. The missionary agreed to try it. When the pilot said, "Pull this lever," he pulled that lever. When the pilot said, "Push this gear," he pushed that gear and so on.

"And sure enough," my friend beamed, "as long as I obeyed that pilot's every instruction, I was free to fly!"

My brother, the missionary, is right. My life is like that now. As long as I live every moment in obedience to the will of Christ – I am free to fly.

What are some of the things which rob Christians of their freedom? Surely, as we mention elsewhere in this book, *worry* is one of our most constant jailers. I believe that during the time we are worrying, we are actually atheistic. Either we believe Jesus Christ or we do not. He said, "I have overcome the world." Did He? Or is He playing a fiendish, cosmic prank upon us? I have, for a year or more, permitted myself the luxury of worry for five minutes at a time and no more. At the end of five minutes, if I am still worried, I go to the nearest mirror, look myself right in the eye and say, "This tremendous thing which worries you is beyond solution. Especially is it too hard for Jesus Christ to handle." Usually, I am restraining a laugh by that time, and when I let it go, the tears of gratitude come with the laugh, and I turn my eyes gladly back upon the face of Him who *gave* me a foolproof "worry-tree" in His Own Cross.

Worry, and fear and self-pity and bitterness and resentment and jealousy and temper and so forth and so forth and so forth can and *do* fence Christians in and prevent them from capering in the freedom Christ died to give us.

He died to set the alcoholic free from the bottle, and the dope addict free from the needle, but they are in the minority, and I wonder often at those of us who go about trying to save alcoholics when we are just as shackled to our sins of the spirit in the eyes of Him who *wants* us to be free.

I have discovered that God's spiritual laws are equally as reliable as His physical laws. If I jump out of a fourteen story window, I don't *break* the law of gravity. I just *illustrate* it. When we disobey God's laws, we don't break those laws. They're unbreakable. We simply illustrate them, as we break ourselves *over* those laws. A pilot who defies the laws of aviation crashes to the earth. He is no longer free to fly. Is the analogy so difficult to apply? Can we not see the freedom in obedience to Christ? Is Jesus Christ a God of His Word, or is He trying to confuse us?

I believe Him. And Jesus Himself said: "If the Son . . . shall make you free, ye shall be free indeed." The Son made me free; free to caper safely and unrestrainedly for the first time in my life, because I am *possessed* by the Holy Spirit of the One who created in me that longing for freedom. The Son of God has made me free, and I am free indeed.

14.

Are You in Love?

ARE YOU IN LOVE? Has your heart been touched by the hand of Him who alone knows the deeps of your heart? And has your heart responded? Has it responded to His voice? Has it been transformed by His touch? Has your heart been laid against His heart, there to stay forever?

Are you in love with the Creator of your heart? Are you in love with the Lover of your soul? Is He your Beloved and are you His? Now, this minute . . . tomorrow morning . . . tomorrow night and forever?

I am in love, and the plan of my love is very simple. To some it could be called my theology. To me it is simply the pattern of love. This is the pattern:

I belong to Christ and He belongs to me.

If you are not in love with Christ as you read these lines, surely you have been in love with someone in your life. And so you will know that when two are in love, the only true happiness for those two comes from being together. If we are separated from the one we love and know the time of reunion is near, don't we count the weeks, then the days, then the hours and then the minutes until we are together again? Did not Jesus pray that we would be one with Him as He is one with the Father? That is the measure of His love for us. He wants not just to be near us, but to be *one* with us. And by His blessed Holy Spirit, He can literally indwell me. By His Holy Spirit, He can literally indwell *you*. He can be your Beloved and you can be His. He wants it that way. Do you?

Jesus of Nazareth, risen from the grave, went to sit at the right hand of the Father in heaven. But, oh, my soul trembles and my heart leaps at the wonder of knowing that although Jesus no longer walks the earth as the Man-God, He can still be present in an even more intimate and deeper sense through the person of His Holy Spirit within me. Out of the chaos of a hectic day, through the tense stillness of a sleepless night, the Voice within me whispers, "Peace, be still . . . I will never leave thee, nor forsake thee." In the midst of weeping, my broken heart is touched by the hand of Him who reminds me, "Lo, I am with you always . . . Let not your heart be troubled . . ."

How little we seem to know about love. How often we confuse love with lust or affection or self-love. Our divorce courts are crowded with men and women who want to be rid of each other because the other person didn't turn out to be the kind of ego-inflater he or she had promised to be. Men and women "fall in love" with their own ideas of what the other person should be. They "fall in love" with only the facets of the loved one's personality which happen to please them. I know this is true. In my B.C. days I was very "loving" to my friends who pleased me. So many tragic times we fall in love for what *we* can get from the relationship.

Close, constant contact with the One who *is* love shows us to our shame that love is giving and not receiving. I honestly believe I loved only one living creature unselfishly before Jesus Christ transformed me. I loved my English bulldog with as nearly an unselfish love as my unregenerate nature could muster. And her love for me? It charmed my life. It gave me, many times, a reason for waking up in the morning. I could desert her for hours, stay away from home until dawn, and instead of barking at me and taking me apart in fury when I finally came home, my doggy just about ate me up with joy because I had come back to her at last.

She taught me something about love. My mother's faith in me through the years taught me more about love. My father's loyalty to me no matter what he found out about me taught me still more about love. My brother's devotion to me in spite of the different worlds in which we lived taught me about love. But not until I met Jesus Christ face to face, did I meet Love as it was divinely created.

Divine love: There are no words to enlarge upon it. Nothing begins to describe it. It is complete in itself. It is – divine love. It has transformed my *self*-love into *other*-love. It has shown me the freedom of pouring myself out at the feet of Him who poured Himself out for me on the Cross. It has touched and transformed my possessiveness into a passion for being possessed by Christ. It has given me the freedom of not *needing* to love myself anymore. He loves me so much, I have no need for self-love, and this sets me free from self-pity, and self-defense, and self-assertion. If I am asked to go the second mile, I am free now to go gladly, knowing that en route, He will press even closer and bind me ever more securely to Himself in divine love.

I wonder at the men and women who follow the chilly reasoning of the cults which propagate the love *principle*. When a child wants its mother, it doesn't want the mother *principle*. It wants its mother's *arms*.

When my heart longs for the God for whom it was created, I do not want the God *principle*. I want the person of God. I want the divine Son of God, Jesus Christ.

When I long for love, I could not be satisfied with the love *principle.* I want the everlasting arms of my Redeemer beneath me.

We must *surrender* ourselves utterly, we must *yield* ourselves completely. And yet, there is another word which I like even better than "yield" or "surrender." That word is "respond." It implies that He needs the response of *my* love to Him. It makes me feel needed. There is no sweeter emotion in all of life than to feel needed by one's beloved. My Beloved needs me and I need Him.

This same Beloved needs you, too. Does not your heart cry for Him? And will it not continue to cry out for Him until it comes to rest against His heart forever?

15.

Are You Satisfied?

ARE YOU SATISFIED and filled, or are you hungry and longing for more and still more of the wonder you have found in Jesus Christ? At first thought, it would seem that the Christian should answer, "Yes, I am completely satisfied." And when the disciple is one with his Master, truly he *is* satisfied. But still he longs for more.

We will return to this aspect of satisfaction in a moment, after we have thought together about the restless kind of dissatisfaction which seems to haunt the heart at night and nip at the heels at noon. So many nervous, jittery Christians dodge through life in much the same tense manner as the non-believer, who must make a go of things by his own wits.

As we consider this tormenting dissatisfaction, we must keep it separated from the healthy hunger about which we will speak later on. If you are nervous, if your spiritual cup is dry, if it has been a long, long time since you have had anything to shout about where your Christian life is concerned, face yourself honestly under the searching eyes of Him who promised to fill the hungry with good things. If you are not filled, could it be that God has gone back on

His promise to you? Did He promise to fill you with good things and then did He get busy with some other celestial undertaking and forget all about you? Did He run out of living water before He reached your empty cup? If I am cross and restless and dissatisfied, does God have too many children to bless so that I can only reason that He must not be able to get around to blessing me today?

Does the Christ who said, "If any man thirst, let him come unto me, and drink," mean to go on depriving me of water for my spiritual life? Am I to go on worrying and fretting and stewing? Are you to go on being anxious and jealous and bitter? Are we to go on feeling sorry for ourselves because all around us others are bubbling over with living water and eating the bread of life?

Now, wait a minute . . . let's examine our side of the agreement. Assuming that we have made an eternal transaction with God on the basis of His redemption and have been reborn and given the power to become sons of God, are we keeping our side of the bargain? Are we spending enough time in the presence of God in silent adoration of Him? Are we feeding our minds and our hearts on the spiritual food in His Holy Scriptures? Are we working for God? Are we spending ourselves for Him? Are we "feeding His sheep"?

Are we?

Or, are we expecting a one hundred percent return from a twenty-five percent investment of ourselves? Of our time? Of our energy? Of our love? Frankly, I can't think of any person on earth who must be more miserable, more restless and more dissatisfied than a part-time, twenty-five percent Christian. If a man has just a little bit of religion, he can no longer enjoy the world's pleasures. He sits in abject misery in the midst of old worldly surroundings where once he reveled and where now he squirms. He sits in church or in a group with victorious, happy Christians and also – squirms. No matter where the poor fellow goes, he is a misfit. He is neither worldly nor Christian. He is divided. He lives in perpetual conflict. He is dissatisfied. And *only* a complete one hundred percent yielding of his life into the hands of the living Christ can calm his conflict, can unify him into one person again – a whole person, who can move toward a goal once more powered by the Dynamo of God, a man united within himself and with his Creator, a man at peace.

If you are restless and dissatisfied, no doubt you are two people trying to live one life. And it's a losing effort, until you unite *all* of you with *all* of Christ.

But what of those of us who are not *dis*satisfied, but who seem to be perpetually *un*satisfied? Is this good? Yes, this is healthy and a sign that we can be filled. We do not really enjoy a good dinner unless we are hungry, do we? So, if you are hungry for more and more of Jesus Christ, rejoice! The pains of hunger are His doing, I believe. He alone can make us want more of Him. He alone can create the hunger within us, just as He alone can satisfy that hunger.

It is very easy for the enemy to disturb us with anxiety over our spiritual condition when those healthy, normal hunger pains begin. He tells us that they are spiritual sickness, spiritual disease. We believe him and become discouraged, and he has the time of his evil life laughing at us as we writhe and agonize before God, begging to be filled when all we really need is to feast on Jesus Christ, the bread of life.

Are you unsatisfied? Are you still hungry? Good. Our Lord does not permit a single need in His children which He Himself cannot and will not fill. He longs to fill us with good things. The good things of the Lord stack up on the back stairs of our souls because we simply do not take them.

Let us rejoice in our hunger, all we who are children of

God, because He wants to feed His hungry children upon Himself, the eternal bread of life.

Isn't it wonderful to be hungry when we can feast on Jesus?

16.

Are You Worried?

ARE YOU WORRIED? How much time do you you spend each day worrying? How much time do you spend being afraid? Literally millions and millions of men and women are haunted night and day by fears, are nagged night and day by worry. For these millions life is one long desperate struggle; one long, futile search for some kind of peace of mind. Pitifully few ever find it.

What is worry? I have found two favorite definitions: "Worry is a cycle of inefficient thought whirling around a center of fear." Read and reread that definition, and its truth will make *you* stop short. First, because we all know of a certainty that worry does produce *inefficiency*. A worried mind is never an efficient mind. Then, the very use of the word "whirling" describes the usual behavior of one who worries. Move on in the definition now. "Whirling" around what? The wrong center. "Whirling around a center of *fear*."

"Fear thou not; for I am with thee . . . I will never leave thee, nor forsake thee."

Are we as Christians supposed to have Jesus Christ in the very *center* of our lives? Then, how is it that *we*, too, are guilty of "inefficient thought whirling around a center of *fear*"?

Another provocative definition of worry goes like this: "Worry is a chronic process of making mountains out of molehills." A Christian woman once looked a friend of mine right in the eye and said sincerely: "Well, if I don't worry, who'll hold things together?"

"Fear not; for, behold, I bring you good tidings of great joy . . . I will never leave thee, nor forsake thee."

With Jesus Christ in the center of our lives, how is it that we continue to worry?

Medical science has proved that literally thousands of illnesses are caused directly from worry and tension and anxiety. American Medical Association statistics tell us that well over *sixty percent* of *all* illness is caused by emotional, mental or spiritual disturbances. We know these things, and yet we continue to worry. Even Christians continue to worry. Our churches are pathetically populated with anxious Christians. *Nervous* Christians clutching doggedly and grimly at their doctrines and their problems instead of becoming "as little children" and resting in the Lord they profess to follow. Why do we do this? Isn't our faith big enough to hold us? Isn't our Lord strong enough to carry our burdens? Must we continue to worry them out ourselves?

"Come unto me, all ye that labour and are heavy laden [with fears and anxieties and worries], and I will give you rest."

We ask: *Is* there a *way out?* Is there a *way* out of fear and anxiety and worry for the tied-up human beings in this old world?

Coming home one night on a local train, I noticed a national magazine on the newsstand in the station. On its cover were splashed these words: NEW DRUGS TO EASE FEAR AND WORRY! I bought the magazine, and found that sure enough, science is gingerly offering a new drug called mephenesin which does, in many cases, offer blessed relaxation from nervous tension. The drug has aided in the improvement of patients with high blood pressure, heart trouble, alcoholism, asthma, etc. It has subdued that demon companion of the anxious – insomnia. A God-sent drug for a certainty. *But,* the article had a feeble pay-off. Science freely admits that this "anxiety fighter" (mephenesin) holds but one promise: It can show the victim what real relief from tension is. It said in effect that once having experienced the incomparable feeling of complete release and relaxation, many people will be able to go on from there to *achieve* true peace of mind and body.

This last statement made me want to sit right down and cry. One would think that people had to be talked into wanting relief from fear and worry and anxiety. That they only had to be convinced that they should try for it! Instead of sitting down to cry, however, I decided to write about this problem.

What have we said? "Worry is a cycle of inefficient thought whirling around a *center of fear.*" We have said that even Christians worry.

Now we ask some questions. Are not Christians supposed to have *Jesus Christ* in the center of their lives? And if so, how can *fear* be there too?

"Let not your heart be troubled . . . I am the good shepherd."

How can we as Christians worry about the fulfillment of our needs? How can we worry about financial matters? About clothes? About bank accounts? If our God is a God of His Word, how do we dare worry?

"Therefore I say unto you, Take no thought for your life, what ye shall eat, or what ye shall drink; nor yet for your body, what ye shall put on . . . Behold the fowls of the air; for they sow not, neither do they reap, nor gather into barns [bank accounts]; yet your heavenly Father feedeth them. Are ye not much better than they?"

Christians who worry must simply be Christians who have not yet gone the second half of the way with Jesus Christ. Christians are the only people on the face of this earth who can possibly escape worry; but only those Christians can escape who are willing to go the *second half* with Jesus, and say, "Yes, Lord, I have *You*, but more important *You* have me!" Those Christians have Jesus Christ straight and tall in the very *center* of their lives. Worry with them is an impossibility. A little boy doesn't worry if he's holding his father's hand, does he?

For our country and for us, the only *way out* of our inner turmoil of confusion and anxiety and worry and fear is the way of Jesus Christ who said: "Come unto me . . . and I will give you rest . . . Lo, I am with you alway . . ."

If we admit to spending even half an hour a day in worry, can't we promise our Lord we'll spend that half hour looking into His wonderful face, while standing steadfastly on His promise, "Seek ye first the kingdom of God, and his righteousness; and all these things [about which you worry] shall be added unto you"?

Jesus Christ is a God of His word. I know. I have tried Him and have found Him faithful. I have problems, yes. Some days they seem to come thicker than snowflakes in a Chicago blizzard. But thank God, I can honestly say these problems – large and small – *never* turn into *trouble.* I don't keep them long enough. I hand them right over to Jesus, who is always standing by waiting to take them. Standing by, keeping His promise:

"Lo, I am with you alway . . ."

17.

"Learn of Me"

If, for some fantastic reason, I were to be suddenly forever deprived of every other passage in the Bible save one, I believe I would choose the last three verses of the eleventh chapter of the Gospel of Saint Matthew:

"Come unto me, all ye that labour and are heavy laden, and I will give you rest. Take my yoke upon you, and learn of me; for I am meek and lowly in heart: and ye shall find rest unto your souls. For my yoke is easy, and my burden is light."

In the Scofield Reference Bible, these three verses are called, "The new message of Jesus: personal discipleship." And since it is this all-compelling personal discipleship which must dominate our lives, if we are to be Christian in the true sense of the word, I feel a deep desire to share a few of my own somewhat recent discoveries concerning one particular line of this wonderful message of Jesus.

The everlasting invitation, "Come unto me, all ye that labour and are heavy laden, and I will give you rest," is a heart-call which no man or woman can resist, once his or her heart has truly been opened to it. But we would look now at the next line: "Take my yoke upon you, and *learn of me.*" A strong childhood memory of having heard that "take my yoke upon you" portion gave me the altogether backward, but unfortunately lasting, impression that the "yoke" of Jesus Christ was a burden in itself. A moment's thought will show how stupid an impression that was. Yokes are devices to lighten burdens. Jesus knew all about yokes, because He must have made them, many of them, with His own hands in the carpenter's shop. He knew they *helped* rather than hindered.

But leaving the "yoke," let's look squarely at the end of that sentence – "learn of me." A direct command of our Lord – "learn of me." As a new Christian, I am wide-eyed with wonder at the prospect of a lifetime . . . an eternity stretching ahead in which I will be able to learn of Him who so completely and wondrously transformed my life – top to bottom, inside and out. After thirty-three years of squeezing dry every situation and exhausting almost every person, I am overcome with adoration of a Lord whom I know I can never exhaust, and who not only says, "Learn of me," but helps me in the learning.

What is it to learn of Jesus Christ? In the beginning of my Christian experience I was convinced I knew all about Him. With a great sweeping gesture of abandon, I "sold all" and flung myself after Him, I thought! Now, I see that I didn't know Him at all. Quite suddenly He had invaded me, but I was still too blinded by my own "light" to see His face. Then, a little later on, when my own light began to die out, I was too dazzled by His light to see *His face* at all.

When we begin to be puzzled by Jesus Christ, I believe that is good. It is doubtful that He would ever turn out to be like our conception of Him. How could we conceive a Lord whose face is "set like a flint" and who stands like "an angel with tears in his eyes" at one and the same time? How could we conceive a Lord who "hath torn and [yet] will heal us? [Who] hath smitten, and [yet] will bind us up?" At these times of utter dismay about Jesus Christ, we feel we are being drowned in darkness. We begin to realize that there is a great distance between Jesus Christ and us. He is up ahead. We must run faster. We must pray more. We must spend more time with Him. Somehow, O God, somehow we must get closer to Jesus Christ! He is up ahead. He is up ahead. We cannot reach Him, and yet He said:

"Learn of me!"

"How can I learn of you, Lord? Where will I begin?"

"If any man will come after me, let him deny himself, take up his cross daily, and follow me."

My Lord's answer: "Deny yourself, take up *your* cross daily, and follow me." Hard? Yes. Without His grace and His strength it is impossible. *With* Him "all things are possible." And delightful and greatly to be desired.

Even a cross? Yes. Because of His Cross our "cross" can be a joyful thing. Can there be joy in pain and suffering? For the true disciple of Jesus Christ, yes. But *only* for the Christian can this be so, because *only* the Gospel of Christ has a direct and effective way of dealing with suffering. By the grace and because of the suffering of Jesus Christ, the Christian is enabled not just to endure suffering; he can *use* it.

This is one of the recent things I have learned about Jesus Christ, in my somewhat stumbling efforts to obey Him when He says insistently: "Learn of me." On the next pages we will speak more of the way out of suffering. Not by escape, not by denial, but by redemptive *use* of whatever blows life deals us. A way out available *only* to those of us who follow the One who "took our sins into His heart and smothered them to death."

18.

What About Suffering?

THERE IS NOTHING so wonderful to the dedicated Christian as to think about Jesus Christ. I spend most of my available free time just *thinking* about Jesus. Nothing shortens a long train ride like thinking about Jesus Christ. Thinking about His gentleness, His almighty meekness, His tears, His deity . . . His lordship . . . His love . . . and all these things leave me sitting happily drowned in His grace. The never-ending, inexhaustible river of His grace. Never flowing away from me. Always flowing toward me. Always toward me . . . coming on, coming on, like a mighty river of love.

Thoughts like these set fire in the hearts of those of us who are His present-day disciples. But, even though Jesus Christ is first in many lives, and even though there are those who say gladly and joyfully, "Though he slay me, yet will I trust in him," still there are more who say, "What has He to offer me when *tragedy* strikes my life?" Or, "I know a wonderful Christian woman whose life has been cut into by tragedy at every turn! How is Christ the way out for her?"

What of all the horrible suffering in the world?

Where is Jesus Christ in all the suffering?

What does He offer as a way out of suffering?

What of the mental anguish inside the churches themselves? What of the wars – mechanized, well-planned – and the bleeding and broken hearts they crush in their iron-hunger for spoils? What of the tragedy in the panic-wake of an earthquake or a volcanic eruption? Of tornadoes and hurricanes and floods? What of physical sicknesses, and the mental anguish that weeps along behind the thousands of funeral processions that move across our world each day? What of the suffering from poverty? From race prejudice? From jealousy? From possessiveness? From doubt? From fear?

What does Jesus Christ have to do with *all* heartbreak? If He is alive, if He really came out of that tomb, what part does He have in the *suffering* of His creatures? Does He simply sit at the right hand of the Father and look down with remote pity on us as we cry out, "Turn thee unto me, and have mercy upon me; for I am desolate and afflicted"? Is this the role of the Son of God in the suffering of His creations? What does Jesus really have to offer when we hear our own hearts break? When we listen to the breaking in the hearts of those we love?

If we worship ourselves as gods, in the time of suffering we turn to the most common form of dealing with it – self-pity. We derive pleasure from feeling sorry for ourselves. There is a touch of this in the fact that almost every man thinks his troubles and sorrows to be the greatest. Self-pity is one way to handle suffering.

Others among us turn to the ancient philosophy of Stoicism. This is the attitude of accepting suffering and inwardly steeling oneself to it. The old bloody-but-unbowed treatment. In a sense, this is admirable, but this very inward steeling turns invariably into hardness of heart. It is Stoic. Not Christian. In fact it is far, far from being Christian, and yet many Christians practice it. Many Christians smile through their tears and mutter between clenched teeth, "Well, I'll take it if it *kills* me! This thing won't get *me* down!" In such an attitude there is a touch of pathetic bravado, but not of genuine Christianity.

Buddha dealt with suffering and sin by declaring, "Existence and suffering are one. There can be no existence without suffering." And since *desire* causes the suffering and the sin, then the only sensible thing to do is to cut the root of desire completely. To lose one's identity in that passionless, actionless state called Nirvana is the Buddhist's way of handling suffering.

The Hindu *denies* the existence of all suffering and sin. He declares himself to be the divine and denies that anything whatever is wrong.

The Moslem lies submissively under the whip hand of sin and suffering and declares all of it to be God's will. This attitude is also shared by many who think themselves completely Christian. How often have you heard someone say in the face of some tragedy: "Well, we'll just have to accept this as God's will"? Christians say this firmly believing that they *know* the nature of Jesus Christ who said: "I am the good shepherd: the good shepherd giveth his life for the sheep." Would a God who said this Himself actively *will* for a baby to be burned to death? No. Suffering is in the world because of sin and evil. Not because it is God's will. And we as Christians must realize and proclaim loudly in our actions that Jesus Christ, our Lord, and *only* Jesus Christ offers a *way out* of suffering. It is a sure *way out* because He and He alone showed us by example how to *use* suffering. Can anything that happens to us be worse than what happened to *Jesus?* And didn't He *use* the Cross to save us?

All other religions deny suffering or dodge it in some manner. The religion of Jesus Christ uses it. The Holy Spirit can and will take your suffering and transform it into good.

This is not idle philosophy. This is fact. Radiant Christians step from prison camps where they have seen their own families murdered before their eyes. How is this possible? Because our Lord accepted the fact of human suffering instead of dodging it. He accepted it and made ready the one and only way of using it redemptively. He did not bring a philosophy. He brought a fact. The fact of Himself. By the very act of allowing His own dear body to be broken on the cross, He took the world's greatest tragedy and turned it triumphantly into the world's greatest testimony! He did not just bear things; He *used* them.

This same Jesus Christ is alive today in all His resurrection power with this practical *way out* of all our human suffering. And He does not expect us to do it alone. He explains little; but if we are willing, He will change anything.

He will take your suffering and your sin into His own heart again right now, and there He will transform it into goodness and joy for you. And best of all, out of your suffering will come a new awareness and new nearness to Jesus, the Christ of God.

I know this to be true. I have discovered it for myself as He showed me how to use a personal tragedy about which I could not even speak. I am grateful that I was not permitted the luxury of sympathy. I *had* to turn to Him alone. Now He has turned my suffering into joy. And scarcely a day goes by that He does not use it at least in some small way.

19.

Listen to What He Has to Say

IF A NEW ACQUAINTANCE asked you the question, "With whom do you live"? what would you reply? Would you say "Oh, I live with my mother, my father and my brother"? Would you say "I live with my husband and my three children?" Or "I live with my wife and four kids, one dog and two canaries"?

No one else? No other Person in your home? Or is He there, but shut away in a dark closet, unable to be a part of the fun in the family, unable to share the warmth around the fireplace in winter, or the cool expectancy of a spring evening daringly spent on the front porch ahead of all the neighbors? Is Jesus Christ shut away in a closet of your home? Can't He come to dinner with you? Can't He converse with you? Is He being deprived of all the *joy* in your *home?* If this is true, then how can we expect to be able to remember where we've hidden Him when *tragedy* strikes our home?

Jesus Himself said: "Learn of me." How can we learn of someone whom we never see? With whom we never have intimate conversation? With whom we never laugh? *To whom we never listen?*

Who is this Jesus Christ who dared to say: "I am the way, the truth, and the life"? Who is this Jesus Christ whom we declare to be the only way out?

"I am the Lord . . . Look unto me, and be ye saved, all the ends of the earth: for I am God, and there is none else." A few short years ago, before my conversion to Jesus Christ, I would have argued: "But how do I know He is God? How do I know?"

"Be still, and know that I am God."

"Be *still*, and know that I am God . . . Learn of me." It is my observation that few Christians take time to be silent and listen to God. How can we obey Him if we do not hear His voice? The Scriptures give us a general plan for guidance, and surely we should take no step which in any way contradicts God's inspired written Word. But, what of the particular times of confusion and indecision which spring from particular circumstances in our own individual lives? The only possible way we can be sure that we are obeying God in these instances is to know Him. To know His character. To know God Himself, as He has revealed Himself through the person of our Saviour and our Lord, Jesus Christ. We can learn much about Jesus Christ personally from learning what He has done in other lives. And yet, this gives us only what the study of theology gives us – knowledge of things *about* Jesus. I would know Him personally. I *must* know Him personally. And so I obey Him when He says: "Be still, and know that I am God."

From the very first morning following my conversion to Jesus Christ, October 2, 1949, I have faithfully kept a "quiet time." I read the Bible, perhaps some devotional book other than the Bible, and then sit for at least half an hour in silence before God. I have been in the homes of ministers during the past two years where I was privileged to share the morning devotions before catching a train. The procedure went something like this: The minister or his wife read from the Scriptures, perhaps one of the children sang, perhaps we all sang (there can never be too much singing!), then usually the minister prayed. And then? Well, then he got briskly to his feet and said, "Now let's be about the business of the day!" I do not mean this in a critical spirit. I am simply puzzled. Because I could not . . . would not *dare* face a day without the fresh infilling of the Holy Spirit during that time of being *quiet* before God when it is morning.

When we go to a doctor we sit down before him and tell him what hurts us. We tell him the symptoms. We ask his advice. *Then* what do we do? Do we dash out the door already intent upon our next bit of business, pleading with the doctor to help us after we are well out of his sight, perhaps down on the street hailing a taxi or waiting for a bus? No, we wait quietly for the doctor's advice. We not only wait for it, we *expect* it. Can he cure our ailment if we don't hear his diagnosis and his remedy?

I think the analogy is apparent. I prayed earnestly for a year for the salvation of one very dear friend, and then one day God managed to get through my much talking with a divine nudge to "Be still, and know that I am God." I fell silent finally. I waited. And in a day or so I realized full well that I had many restitutions to make before that friend could possibly see Jesus Christ through me. Since I was the only plausible link between her and God, I had to set about making those painful restitutions at once.

Surely we can come to know Jesus Christ personally in no better way than being quiet before Him. Time spent in feeding our inward lives with His lovely presence will ultimately make it possible for us to carry this inner life out into the market place. Time spent in silence before God teaches us what it really means to "pray without ceasing." We come to live on two levels at once. The calm of the deep, quiet, unchanging inner level where we are Christ's and Christ is God's, where the pool of His peace is never disturbed by any tornadoes blowing from without, will begin to be felt in the bustle and turmoil of our exterior lives. Those who spend time with us will not only know that we "have been with Jesus," but that we *are* with Jesus. Our very lives will speak for Him, because the living God will speak through our lives to an anguished, frightened world: "Come unto me . . . Look unto me, and be ye saved . . . I and my Father are one . . . be still, and know that I am God."

20.

"I Am the Door" (I)

I FIND ONE FRAGMENT of Scripture coming again and again, and so I will set down this fragment, and allow it to lead us down still another path of discoveries about Jesus.

"I am the door: by me if any man enter in, he shall be saved, and shall go in and out, and find pasture . . . Verily, verily, I say unto you, He that entereth not by the door into the sheepfold, but climbeth up some other way . . ."

What other *ways* are there? How do we dare choose another way beside the way of the One who declared and got a world to believe that "I am the way, the truth, and the life"? How do we dare go against the One who also declared: "I am the door"?

What other ways of facing life are there? Too many to list. But commonly, there is the way of *resentment.* There is the way of *escape mechanisms.* There is the way of *self-defense.* There is the way of *materialism.* There is the way of *fear.* There is the way of *pleasure.* But do these ways lead to a victorious life? No, they lead to – nothing. They are dead-end ways. They are blind alleys. And yet we, the blind, lead the blind up and down these alleys daily, refusing the *one* way out. Refusing even to try the door.

The famous nerve specialist, Dr. Walter Alvarez, says: "I often tell patients that they cannot afford to carry grudges or maintain hates or resentments. Such things can make them ill and can certainly tire them out. I once saw a man kill himself, inch by inch, simply by thinking of nothing but hatred of a relative who had sued him. Within a year or two he was dead." God has fashioned us for love. Not hate. For love. Not resentment. "Love is our native air." Anything else is poison. Surely the way of resentment is a rough road with a dead-end. The only *way out* of resentment permanently is by the cleansing and redemption of the One who offers Himself as the door.

Then there are the ways of *escape mechanisms.* Among those ways most struggled along are the winding, endless catacombs of *alcoholism* and *sensationalism.* Just as one drink for the alcoholic usually leads to two, so one sensation tried leads to boredom and the pursuit of still another sensation. The door out of those twisting tunnels of darkness? There is only one way . . . one door of release. Jesus tells us: "I am the way . . . I am the door."

There is another well-traveled way with a dead-end: the way of *self-defense.* "I've got a right to stick up for my rights!" But Jesus said: "He that findeth his life shall lose it: and he that loseth his life for my sake shall find it." We stand our ground and scream: "I'll fight for my rights!" Christ says: "If any man will sue thee at the law, and take away thy coat, let him have thy cloak also."

Another popular way of life is the way of *materialism.* We are a material-mad race of people. Build, increase, expand, pile up, hoard. More and more and more. "If we can just make enough money to – to – !" Jesus said: "Sell that ye have, and give alms; provide yourselves bags which wax not old, a treasure in the heavens that faileth not, where no thief approacheth, neither moth corrupteth."

Still another way is the shadowy way of *fear.* No one consciously chooses this way. But anyone can leave it behind forever. An ancient Persian saying contends: "Worry eats up the human flesh." Medical science says, "So does fear." In Mark 4:19 we see that: "The cares of this world . . . choke the word, and it becometh unfruitful." One writer declares, "Not only do care and fear and worry 'choke the word,' they choke the person too!" It is a well-known medical fact that fear-ridden patients are easily choked. They are shallow breathers. What is the way out of the way of fear? There is only one. The One who declared: "*Fear* not, little flock; for it is your Father's good pleasure to give you the kingdom."

There is also the *way of pleasure.* This so-called way leads perhaps more quickly and more heartbreakingly to a dead-end than any other. I know. I tried it for some fifteen years. Tried it skillfully. Carefully. Expensively. Imaginatively. Diligently. And ultimately – despairingly. The *pursuit of pleasure* occupies the minds and spare hours and energies of nine out of ten men, women and children in this vast land of ours. No one loves a good time more than I do. And I thank God that at last . . . at long last, I have learned the art of having a good time "in the midst of." A trip to a particular place no longer guarantees a happy vacation for me. I will have joy and the "peace that passes all understanding" if my vacation doesn't pan out as I have planned it in any detail. Why? Because Jesus will be wherever I am . . . giving His joy minute by minute by minute . . . "in the midst of."

People shout: "We wanta' have fun our way!" Jesus says: "These things have I spoken unto you, that *my* joy might remain in you, and that your joy might be full."

"These things have I spoken unto you . . . I am the door

. . . no man cometh to the Father but by me . . . I am the door . . . I am the way, the truth, and the life."

We who have tried to climb up some other way have found unmistakably and forever . . . that Jesus Christ *meant* every word He said.

21.

"I Am the Door" (II)

JESUS SAID: "I am the door." What did He mean? Obviously He meant much more than we know about. But think for a moment about doors themselves. We think of a door as an article which opens *into* or out of something. A door leads from something to something. A doorway leads from one room to another. Jesus said: "I am the door." He also said: "I am the way." Jesus Christ, then, unless He lied, actually leads from one state to another. We can agree on this.

What, according to psychologists (*and* according to what we know of ourselves) do we, as human beings, fear or dread above all other phenomena? What would we avoid if we could? Here are four major "dreads" which, if man could pass through, or avoid, he would, I believe, be free from most of his fear:

First, *death*. We fear death for many reasons. God has planted in every living thing the desire to live. Even the tiniest bug will struggle for life when faced with death. Injured men will crawl for miles for life-saving aid, fearing, dreading death. Psychologists say, "Every man in his right mind wants life." And yet, there is nothing . . . nothing so certain, so absolutely inevitable as *death.* Birth may fail. Never death. *But wait* . . .

" . . . whosoever believeth in *him* should not perish, but have *everlasting* life."

If we are to believe Jesus Christ, if we are to believe the inspired word of God as we read it in His Word, the Holy Bible, we are faced with a startling statement: "I am the door . . . I am the way . . . [to] everlasting life"!

Did Jesus Christ mean what He said? Was it all true? *Is* it still true? If it is not, He was the most shocking deceiver who ever walked this earth. But He was not. It is true.

From my own experience, I know I have found the door which leads from *death* into *eternal life.* I have been found by the One who said: "I am the resurrection and the life." Jesus cancels the fear of *death* by His *life.*

We look now at dread number two, *failure, defeat.* No one wants to be a failure. There is nothing to celebrate in failure. Celebrations go with victories. No one wants or seeks failure . . . and society as a whole does not love a man who is a failure. We fear *failure.* We dread *defeat.* The alcoholic who sits dejectedly before his half empty bottle, after having sworn off forever, knows the abject humility and pain of *defeat.* The mother who watches her son being led away to prison knows the heartbreak of personal failure. The schoolboy lags behind his classmates as they leave for home the last day of school; the blood is pounding in his head from the humiliation he feels because *his* report card reads: Failure. No one walks through life without major *and* minor defeats and failures. But wait . . .

Jesus said: "I have overcome the world." And dear aging John, the disciple Jesus loved, drew on the strength of His Lord to declare: "Whosoever believeth that Jesus is the Christ is born of God . . . [and] whatsoever is born of God overcometh the world: and this is the victory that overcometh the world, even our faith." Surely, Jesus Christ *is* the door from *defeat* to victory.

Dread number three is the dread of *bondage.* Of not being *free.* America is built upon the belief in freedom. And yet, no nation can guarantee personal freedom to its people. Personal freedom from the bondage of self and sin and the inevitable circumstances of life *must* come from *above* and be worked out *within* each individual life. We have seen radiant Christians chained to their wheel chairs. We have been guided by radiant Christians with sightless eyes. We have watched bed-ridden Christians "mount up with wings as eagles." Why? How? Because they have walked by faith through the door to – freedom.

Jesus said: "If the Son . . . shall make you free, ye shall be free indeed."

Lastly, man's fear and dread of *insecurity* can rule and ruin his entire life. There are two ways of meeting this fear on the human level. We can lay up material security, or we can deny the need for it. Both ways are false. But the man or woman who, like Paul, has "learned both to abound and to be in want" is truly free of this black dread of insecurity forever.

. . . When you have stopped reading, I beg you to spend several minutes in quiet contemplation before this One who dares to say: "I am the door" which leads *away* from *defeat, bondage, insecurity* and *death,* and "I am the way" which leads *to* victory, freedom, security and eternal life.

22.

Where Is Jesus Christ?

WHERE IS JESUS CHRIST?

Where would one find Him in your life? Where do *you* find Him? Do you have to travel to some particular place? Do you have to do some particular thing?

Where do you go to find Jesus? Where do you go to be sure of the presence of God? In all ages, religion has been associated with sacred places. Thousands drag their sick and weary bodies to the banks of the Ganges river, so they may die in sight of this sacred stream. A friend of mine, a missionary, once saw a Mohammedan saying his prayers on a train. The Mohammedan knelt upon his prayer mat on the floor of the train and tried to face toward Mecca. I say he *tried* because the train happened to be spiralling up a twisting mountain track, and the poor Mohammedan had to resort to a compass placed on the floor in front of him so that he could keep turning his body in a rather frantic effort to keep facing the holy place.

Does this make you smile? Well, where do *you* find Jesus? How do *you* contact God?

You may have read, as I have, of the Indians of Latin

America who take long pilgrimages to a sacred shrine made in the image of Christ. But as they leave, they are heard to cry: "Adios, Christos! Adios, Christos!" – "Good-bye, Christ! Good-bye, Christ!"

They leave Christ standing there trapped in that sacred shrine, as they walk away tearfully waving good-bye to the One who died that they might *be one* with Him forever.

Where do you find Jesus Christ? In church you say? Yes, so do I. But what about the moment when you walk out the front door of your church and down the steps toward home? Does Jesus go along with you, or do you leave Him behind – trapped in the stained glass window or shut until next week between the airless pages of the Psalter resting in the church pew where you sat?

Before I received Jesus Christ as my Saviour and Lord I thought of these two words, "sacred" and "secular," as being poles apart. And now, when I look about at God's children from within the warm, safe encirclement of His everlasting arms, I am hurt and many times bewildered that so many of His followers only follow Him part of the way. The dividing line between their *sacred* and their *secular* is wide and sometimes uncrossable.

I knew the utter darkness of a life of atheism. I am Christ's now. I am spared the struggle of indecision, the agony of choosing and the throes of the double-walk. I simply follow Jesus and take my strength from His Holy Spirit which dwells within me. I tremble at the turmoil which rushes toward me like a black and angry monster when I step off the "holy highway" of obedience to Christ.

I wonder and sometimes marvel at the human fortitude of Christian believers who manage to live both a secular and a sacred life. I marvel at those who can leap back and forth across that darksome gap between trips to church from week to week. I do not speak of worldly indulgences now;

I merely speak of those who leave Jesus Christ in the pews when they leave their churches.

I have found Jesus Christ to be directly interested and quite personally involved with me in every line I write. I am firmly convinced that Jesus Christ is interested in our vacation plans, our recreation time, our fun. I have a devout friend who lives in His presence from minute to minute, who once had his early morning devotions broken while on a fishing trip. A large fish nearly jerked the pole out of his hand. He landed the fish, and went on with his prayer. "There didn't seem to be a real interruption," he said later. "The Lord was interested in my fishing trip." I believe this. This man belongs to Christ completely. Why wouldn't Christ be interested in his fishing trip? Can't we take God into everything? To take Him into everything does not mean that we lower *Him;* it merely means that we *lift our lives!* To take God into our pleasures does not mean that we make Him commonplace. I believe it means that we allow Him to make our pleasure *un*common.

As I write these words I am beginning the fourth year of my walk with Jesus Christ. I have discovered many things. I have been given a completely new life. Not one of the least exciting discoveries I have made, however, is this: When I determined to take Christ into my every pleasure, I found the *one sure way of finding out* just what a Christian can and cannot do and still remain true to the Person whom he follows!

And so, as an extremely happy and joy-filled and delighted Christian of three years (at this writing), I want to go on record as saying that I believe no Christian has a right to take part in *anything* into which he or she cannot walk wholeheartedly with Jesus Christ. We can just toss out the two words "secular" and "sacred" from our vocabulary from now on, and rejoice as we gladly call it *all* – His.

23.

Your Talent, Yes, But You Too

"JESUS CHRIST does not want your talent. He wants *you!*"

I have dashed several young (and not so young) hopefuls full in the face with this seemingly blunt and discouraging statement. I don't enjoy seeing my words wipe smiles away and furrow brows of these would-be Christian writers, actors, musicians, singers, producers, directors, et cetera, ad infinitum. It is embarrassing, in fact, since at the moment I am earning my living as a Christian writer, director and producer.

I cannot, however, but believe this is the truth concerning the question of service: "Jesus Christ does not want your talent. He wants you!" After all, upon facing the matter squarely, doesn't giving yourself entirely to Him *include* your talents too? Now, perhaps you are saying: "Well, what's all the fuss about then? Isn't it all the same in the final analysis?"

No, it is not the same. It is a fearful and dangerous thing, I believe, for a disciple of Christ to decide *how* Christ is to use his or her talents. It would seem that if one is blessed with a lovely voice that he or she should serve God as a singer. Or a writer, if he or she can write. Or as an artist, if he or she can paint. But I am forced, by my own firm conviction and by the results of my own experience, to insist that Jesus meant what He said when He said: "Come unto *me!*"

He didn't say, "Bring your talent unto me." He said, "*You* come yourself!" To me it makes all the difference in the world which comes first. If we bring the talent first – even if we offer it completely – we are holding onto the right to ourselves. If we say, "Lord, here is my lovely singing voice, I would use it for Thee," we are, as a friend of mine says, "making a cosmic errand boy of God." We are directing Him.

But, if we come to Him first, holding out empty hands, offering ourselves *and* the right to ourselves, then and only then can Jesus Christ make *full* use of our talents to the *glory of Himself.*

I know this to be true. I tried it.

Some three years ago, when I surrendered my life into the hands of the living God, I said to myself dramatically (and quite naturally): "You have been a successful writer for ten years in the service of the enemy of God. Now you must give your years of experience and your talent to Christ, perhaps to write *the great* Christian novel!"

I have to smile now, remembering my spiritual blindness in those first, eager days in the kingdom. Jesus Christ knew about the talent. And He knew what use He might have for it – *in the future.* But He also knew that He had a still stubborn, still carnal, still unbroken newborn creature on His hands. She was waving her arms and saying: "I will serve Him with *my* talent," and He was holding her in His hand patiently awaiting the moment when she quieted down enough for Him to get a word in too.

He could not use her talent until He had her completely.

Gradually, over the strange new months of that first year,

as I began to get closer and closer to the person of Jesus, I said less and less about "the great novel." I thought less and less about "writing for God" and more and more about *knowing* Him personally. Slowly this began to dawn on my newly awakened consciousness concerning things as they *are* in the kingdom of God: My business was *not* to serve Jesus Christ. My business was to *belong* to Him utterly and completely and without one single reservation. Then, and only then, could He trust me with His service.

Isn't it easy for us to decide *for* God about how we are to serve Him? Isn't it easy for us to satisfy our own egos by cloaking our personal ambitions in the language of God, and arranging the spectators and the setting to suit our own ideas of our own merits and capabilities?

Yes, it's more than easy. It's *natural*. But the power with which we reckon as Christians is *supernatural*, and so it is not for us to consecrate our gifts to God. They are not ours to give.

Ours is not to decide; ours is to belong. Ours is to do the will of Him we adore. And He said: "If any man will come after me, let him deny himself, take up his cross daily, and follow me."

"Follow *me*," not a particular form of service for which we seem fitted. "Follow *me!*" And we can only follow Him according to His will by drawing ever closer to Him in our daily lives. Not closer to a religion, but closer to the altogether lovely person of Jesus Christ. We cannot please a friend completely unless we know that friend's every wish. And so, let us open our minds and wills and hearts to Him, asking Him, by the Spirit of truth, to teach us more and still more about Him*self*. Because the more we know of Jesus as He is, the less we are concerned with our own personalities except that they be caught up in the light of the personality of the One whom we serve – not for the sake of serving, but because we belong.

You say: "But if I am born with a talent, isn't it just common sense that I use it for God?" No, not necessarily. If common sense had been enough, Jesus would not have had to die.

Is that true? Yes.

If common sense had been enough, Jesus Christ would not have had to die.

24.

Adventure in Holiness

I WANT TO SHARE with you an adventure in holiness which I experienced in the early summer of 1952.

I had, for some months, been anticipating a week-long speaking engagement in three farming towns in Illinois because I looked forward to spending some time with my friend, Mrs. Lorena Galloway, who arranged the tour. Otherwise, to all outward appearances it was to be a fairly routine engagement. But from the first hour, I felt something unusual stirring within, as the streamlined train slipped away from Chicago, across fields planted row on row with new green corn, past quiet towns, bright green patches of forest, and tidy little front yards where women and children looked up from their flowerbed planting to wave at us.

I expected a happy time. I knew the food would be garden-picked and prepared with love; I knew the water would be well-fresh; I knew the people would be warm and the welcome wide. And yet something unusual stirred within me and I wanted to stretch forward in my seat in an effort to help the train along its speeding way. The book I had open kept falling unnoticed to the seat beside me as my eyes were drawn, time after time, away from its pages out toward the wide, blue and white miracle of summer sky overhead. I longed for "eyes that could pierce the skies and look into the Father's eyes" as Jesus' eyes had done when He walked on earth.

I wondered vaguely if I would ever attempt to explain to anyone about this strange stirring, this anticipation beyond what would seem to be the plausible. Time after time I tried to go back to the book, telling myself that I was indeed duller from the heavy round of speaking engagements and writing assignments than I had realized.

. . . And yet, time after time, the book slipped back down to the seat unnoticed and my eyes ached to penetrate the sky which alone remained vast and almost still as the rest of the landscape whirled by. I was moving toward something which I almost feared and yet for which undoubtedly I longed. Was I being "called"?

Now, I can report to you that I was hurtling across more than the seemingly endless stretches of Illinois prairie land. I was hurtling toward an adventure in holiness.

I have heard a complete walk of holy obedience to Jesus Christ described as giving the follower "the naivete which is the yonder side of sophistication." I had longed to obey Jesus literally and truly – to become as a little child. I had seen evidence in the lives of the departed saints, in the transfigured faces of certain contemporary saints that the wholly surrendered, wholly submissive, wholly listening, wholly obedient life is as Thomas Kelly wrote "astonishing in its completeness."

This I had seen. This I believed. And at times my own experience had proven it to me beyond the shadow of any doubt. But . . . only "at times." I would intend fully to remain wholly obedient. Wholly submissive. Wholly trusting. Then an unusually difficult bit of work would come along, or someone with a badly twisted personality would come to me for help; and before I realized what was happening, I had once more taken the reins into my own hands and was bumping along under my own *knowledge* of Christian behavior, spilling the very living water out of the cup I attempted to give to the thirsty person who had come to drink. I was again managing my own universe.

I was once again "making God a cosmic errand boy" in my prayers and was rushing eagerly ahead of Him, tripping over my own spiritual feet as I strove to serve Him – *my way.*

I knew that a Christian's only duty is to belong to Jesus Christ. I knew that. I believed it. And sometimes I lived in that realm of happy freedom, wholly dependent upon Him for days at a time. But . . . those days passed, because my heart was not consistently invaded by His blessed Spirit. Perhaps the reader has another explanation for the spasmodic peace I knew. I believe I had merely been blocking the divine invasion of the person of the Holy Spirit of Jesus Christ.

. . . I rejoice to report that to the best of my knowledge now, the invasion is complete; and it was made via my *heart,* which was newly melted into submissiveness as I lived and ate and laughed and rejoiced and loved among a few of God's totally obedient children who live here and there in various stages of poverty and plenty in and around the three small farming towns of Bushnell, Smithfield and Macomb, Illinois. Words grow stubborn . . . in fact they refuse to be set down in what would inevitably be a futile attempt to explain what happened when my passionate hunger for the bread of life was satisfied at last as I was let into the hearts of the Galloways, Minnie Sims, the Rectors, and their friends . . . to feed with them upon Jesus. With complete singleness of eyes those people are centered down in the One who alone can perform the miracle of the transfigured face and the transformed life. They don't *wonder* about God. They *know* Jesus personally. They live with Him minute by minute in complete obedience as they understand it. They not only possess the Holy Spirit; the Holy Spirit possesses them.

The life of holy obedience is not reserved for a few. If we would survive, it *must not* be limited to a few. It is for for every follower of Jesus Christ to know the pure wonder of the utter simplification and rest that come inevitably when the life has been drenched in power from on high. There are many who will swarm Jesus Christ, but few will *touch* Him. But we must remember that "as many as touched him were made perfectly whole."

25.

The Difference Between "Life" and Life

WE'VE ALL HEARD the expressions, "I want to *live!*" or "A man only *lives* once, so I'm going to make the most of every minute!" I have not only heard both expressions; I have used them time and time again . . . *before* I found out what *life* really means. What *living* really means.

"I am the way, the truth, and the *life*. No man cometh unto the Father but by me . . . whosoever believeth on me, shall have everlasting *life* . . . he who hath the Son hath *life*."

Before grasping the eternity of difference between "life" and *life*, we have a tendency to squeeze the last drop from every experience. A good interlude, such as an absorbing book or an enjoyable concert, or a happy vacation time can make us feel that "life" is good. We hang onto each ephemeral moment of these happy times and say, "If only this could go on – this is really living!"

Well, that *is* living a "life." But we must find *the life*, and "this is life eternal, that they might know thee the only true God, and Jesus Christ whom thou hast sent." And, to *know* God as revealed to us in His Son, Jesus, is to *have* eternal life. A *life*, which is not only for some future time, but a *life* which begins the very instant a man or woman turns the reins of his or her existence over to the Son of God.

At thirty-six years of age, I have finally found that under our own steam – searching about wildly as we may – we cannot *live* through earthly power. Nor through chemical power (including all the artificial stimuli known to mankind). Nor can we *live* through human power: physical, intellectual, emotional or will power. The only power by which we can find life is the power promised by Jesus to all believers . . . that inexhaustible, dynamic enduement of power that comes to us the moment the Holy Spirit comes in to take over in our stead.

Only one or two Christians (including the clergy) have been able to give the writer (a new Christian) a realistic definition of the Holy Spirit. Some theological explanations have stimulated the mind, but I am overjoyed to report that the Holy Spirit Himself has revealed *Himself* to me in a new and vital way. The Holy Spirit has ceased being "It" and has become *He!* The Spirit of truth is come . . . he will guide . . . into all truth.

The Holy Spirit is not a freak of God nor a spasm of the divine nature, nor a pocket edition of Jesus Christ. He is not a mere influence nor the inspiration of a poet or teacher. He is a divine Personality, an almighty Being who has a will, an intellect and a heart. He Himself must live in us or there is no more divine power in us than in others. He Himself must move in us or we are helpless. He Himself must speak through us or else our words will be "as the babbling of fools or the crackling of thorns under a pot."

When Pilgrim started his progress away from the City of Destruction he cried, "Life, Life, more Life!" Too much of our cry today is, "Work, work and more work." Or, "Service, service and more service." Or, "Funds, funds and more funds." Or, "Crowds, crowds and more crowds."

In my own personal life I have discovered as an irrefutable

truth that unless the presence of the Holy Spirit of God goes along with my progress away from my "city of destruction," I will cry helplessly against a canvas sky . . . and hang my highest hopes on no loftier summit than the point of a cardboard moon.

The Holy Spirit manifests Himself in us in the "more abundant life." And life can only be defined as – life. We cannot analyze it, imitate it or create it. A professor at a large western university once took a common squash and put it in a steel case. On the lid of this steel case, he placed a one hundred pound weight. The squash grew and its *life* lifted the hundred pounds. He then put on a two hundred pound weight. The squash lifted the added weight. The professor then put on five hundred pounds of weight. The squash grew and up went the five hundred pounds. Then on went an anvil and a piece of railroad iron. And the life-filled squash plant broke the steel case to pieces!

If God can put that much power in a squash, what amount of power can He put into a disciple of His Son, Jesus Christ? And what potent kind of *life* can we as disciples send out into all the darkened world, if we but turn completely to the *life* for which we were created?

Why *waddle* along through "life" when we can *soar* through *life?*

26.

What Is in the Center of Your Life?

WHAT IS IN THE VERY CENTER of your life? If we follow Jesus Christ, it would seem the answer would be obvious. We should be able to say without hesitation: "Why, Jesus Christ is in the center of my life."

But can we say this and feel certain our statement will stand up under close investigation? As one so lately a member of the pagan world, and as one so deeply concerned that other pagans are allowed to see Christ as He really *is*, and so come into His kingdom joyfully, as I came, I beg of you to look closely at your life as we come to the closing pages of this book of discoveries about the person of Jesus Christ.

On the absolute childlike belief that He meant every word He said, I stake my eternal life on the fact that if Jesus Christ is lifted up – *as He* really *is* – He will draw all men unto Himself! He said He would, and I believe Him. And with this promise of His in our hearts, let us face clearly some of the innocent, unconscious habits of thinking into which Christians fall; habits which turn *away* non-believers when the sincere desire of the Christian's heart is to bring them *into* the wonderful light.

I believe these habits can all be summed up under the heading of "too much self-effort." And this is why I say that we get so carried away with wanting to serve Christ that we leap in and try to do His work for Him. I have spoken at some length earlier about the gentle, simple way in which I was brought into the glorious personal walk with Jesus Christ. And I want to emphasize for the sake of clarity, and for Jesus' sake, that there is *no one set way* of leading a man, woman or child to Christ. Our part is merely to "lift Him up" and let Him do His own work.

In the portion on the viewpoint of Christ, we discussed this in detail. But now, we should look at just a few of the *right* endeavors which we put in the *wrong* places in our Christian lives.

First of all, Jesus did say, "Go ye into all the world and make disciples." And any effort on our behalf to lead another human being into a saving knowledge of Jesus Christ is one of the vital roots of a Christian life. *But,* how many of us put "soul-winning" in the very center of our lives and thus go about tight-lipped and tense, *hiding* Jesus Christ behind our own anxious natures, instead of "lifting Him up"? Again, I ask you to *think* as you read these lines. They can be so easily misread. No one among you thrills more to the pure joy of bringing a stray sheep home to the Shepherd than I do. I know how lonely and lost it feels to be out there in the world without Him. I know what a desperate feeling it is to have the universe end with the top of one's own head. But, if I allow my desire to "win others" to settle in the center of my life, Jesus Christ has to move to the margins. I become tense and nervous when the days go by without my having brought anyone to Christ, and before I know it, I am hiding Him from the world behind my own anxiety.

We must keep Christ Himself in the center.

We need only stay in position to be used. We need only to do as the lilies do. Wouldn't we pity the poor apple blossom that cried to bear an apple of its own effort? But we needn't pity the poor apple blossom, because it is wise enough to stay in position on the branch until the apple is born *through* it.

It is easy for well-meaning, sincere Christians to put soul-winning in the center of their lives, so that Jesus Christ is moved to the margins. But if He is in the center, dominating our thoughts, calming our fears, erasing our anxiety, *balancing* our lives, He will keep His word and draw others unto Himself – *because* of Himself.

It is also easy for well-meaning, sincere Christians to put "witnessing" in the center of their lives. We hear well-intentioned admonitions to witness daily for our Lord. But if I talked about Jesus Christ simply because I thought it was my duty to talk about Him, secretly I'd begin to resent the whole thing in no time. I am not ashamed to admit this. It is a simple fact. On the other hand, when we are so in love with Christ, so completely convinced that even if there were no eternal reward when we leave this earth, *His* is still the most fulfilling, the most exciting, the most joyful way of life, *then* we talk about Him because we just can't help it. I have asked myself this question for many months and at last I can answer it in the *affirmative* with no hesitation:

> *If* for some reason Jesus Christ came to me and said that He had made a big mistake, that there was no eternal reward, and no heaven and no hell – would I still follow Him?

Would you? Can you answer that right now with a quick, uncompromising "Yes"? If you can, then you do not worry about when and where you will be called upon or permitted the chance to witness. You will just talk about Him because you are so full of Him you can't help doing it. I have heard sincere Christians pray for the "opportunity" to witness. Every breath we take is that opportunity. Every cab ride, every dinner out, every bus ride, every guest who drops in, every time the front door bell or the telephone rings – we are swamped with chances to talk about Jesus. Now, I do not mean to imply that we must clench our fists and set our jaws and force a word about Him *every* time we brush another human being. That, in fact, is my point. If we force ourselves to witness, then we are putting our *duty to witness* in the center, and over into the margin of our lives must go our Lord.

Just as we can put service to Christ, to humanity, to our churches in the center, so we can put winning others and witnessing in the center. I believe *all* these are the fruits of *belonging* entirely to the *only* One who has the right to stand forever in the very center of our lives – Jesus Christ.

27.

Easter

When I was a child of about seven or eight, my mother bought a lovely straw Easter bonnet for me. Usually careful in the extreme about the fit of my garments, somehow she slipped up on this particular hat. And the first time I wore it, she asked with tender concern: "Dear, is your new hat too tight for you?"

"No, Mother," I sighed philosophically, "it's all right *after* my ears go to sleep!"

That incident, the memory of my mother conducting the Easter cantata at church, Irving Berlin's song, "Easter Parade," and a passing interest in which of my friends made the Sunday rotogravure on a few Easters in particular, constitute the over-all meaning of the season to me until I was thirty-three years old. Aside from a rather characteristic eccentricity of refusing to buy a new hat until well *after* Easter, because the hoi-polloi bought bonnets at Easter, it was just another commercial holiday which I was asked to note in whatever radio show I happened to be writing in the spring of the year.

Now . . . *every morning is Easter morning to me!* I found

it easy to toss off the above lines of description of Easter B.C. in my life. Words become stubborn now as I struggle to combine them into some semblance of what I have discovered to be the true meaning of this glad time of the year.

First of all, when Easter morning breaks in all its light and glory upon my consciousness, it trails an unmistakable crimson cloud just lifted from the empty cross which my Lord left behind Him in order to "come back" to indwell me. I know His actual presence with me now *only* because He came out of that grave on the first Easter morning. If Jesus, the risen Christ, had not gone to be with the Father, the blessed Comforter – my Lord with me *now* – could not be here. Could not be there with you.

Just as Jesus must have swayed a moment on His wounded feet, as He stood in the mouth of the newly opened grave, adjusting His eyes to the sunlight of His own resurrection, so I sway in wonder at being able to share in this same resurrection today. Just as the nail prints were still in His hands and feet, so the scars of my own crucifixion with Him remind me that I *am* crucified with Christ. And am free because of it. The life I have discovered in Him has scars on it. But they are *glowing* scars because He lives *in me* now that the grave is open and empty.

Do we as Christians *live* every minute of our lives as though we really believe He came out of that tomb that first Easter morning? Do we live as though Easter is a legend or a reality? Do we let the world know that the very same power that brought Jesus Christ *out* of that heavy-shadowed blood and spice encrusted grave that first Easter morning *is operative in us today?* Do we live by the same power of God unto resurrection?

The Mary who loved Him so, Mary of Magdala, occupies a high place in my heart. I might have been that Mary. I love Him enough to have been that Mary. He forgave me for so much and I love Him according to that which I have been forgiven. My heart beats near hers now and I hope to be her close friend throughout eternity as we sit together at His beloved feet . . . pouring out our love before Him forever. I love Him for coming to her ahead of the others that first Easter morning. He did not love her *more*, but she was *there* looking for Him. And He honors those of us who are always seeking for new ways to tell Him of our love. He honors our seeking for more of Himself . . . for the sake of Himself. Mary of Magdala sought Jesus for Himself. She did not seek a blessing from Him. He was and *is* her blessing. As He is my blessing forever. I cannot ask for any other gift from Him. He dwarfs even His own gifts. My heart longs for more and still more of the Giver Himself. And this constant seeking for more of Jesus, for some new glimpse of Him, is one reason why every morning is an Easter morning for me.

And then, too, every morning is Easter morning to me because He lives within me every day. I could not believe in the actual physical resurrection of Jesus Christ *before* it took place in my own life.

I know He is risen now. He is with me minute by minute. My risen Master, my Lord . . . Rabboni! And I, too, go quickly and tell.

28.

I Am His and He Is Mine

I AM HIS AND HE IS MINE. That is my theology. It is very simple and I have discovered to my great and eternal joy that it works.

I did not become a Christian to save myself from eternal damnation. I did not become a Christian to make certain my passage to heaven. I did not think about either hell or heaven when I was being moved within by the Holy Spirit of Jesus Christ. Had I thought about them, I would not have been influenced by them because I did not believe they existed. I believe in them now, but *then* my attention was completely taken up mentally, emotionally and spiritually by the person of Jesus Christ. I was captivated by the One who holds "captivity captive."

I did not pick and choose among the various churches during the time the Holy Spirit bore down upon my brittle heart. I did not think much one way or another about churches. I had not been inside one in almost eighteen years and although I love them now and believe every new Christian *must* unite his life and efforts with some Christian group, at that moment when the Holy Spirit pressed in upon my sin-encrusted consciousness, I did not think of churches. I thought about Christ. And the more I thought about Him, the more real He became to me; and the more real He became, the more I wanted Him to be mine. And then my simple theology came into being. He seemed to say:

"I'll be yours if you'll be mine."

If you have read through this book, you know that my discoveries about the Christian life can be included in one sweeping over-all discovery:

I belong to Him and He belongs to me.

In the person of the Holy Spirit, my Lord is with me and in me as I work and play and laugh and weep and love on the earth. I am one of His sheep. I know His Name. I am His and He is mine.

It is His privilege and right to instruct me to do anything for His sake. I will go anywhere and do anything Jesus Christ asks me to do; and by His grace, I will do it calmly, willingly and quickly, because of who He is. He does not tell me to do something He cannot do.

I do not plead for Him to help me. I simply try to stay in position so He can work and love and serve *through* me. This is very restful for me *and* brings me into a climate of high excitement at one and the same time, since I am allowed to "rest" as His energy pours through me into the tasks He has set to be done.

There is no need for me to wonder whether or not He will get through to me in time to make ends meet. He is here "nearer than breathing and closer than hands and feet" every instant.

From the experience of this moment through which I am living as I write, "I am strengthened mightily by His Spirit in my inner self."

When the press of the crowds and the demands of people in trouble hack at my nerves, He whispers gently in my ear: "Leave them to Me, no one ever gets on My nerves."

When I am inclined to wonder if there will be enough material supply to go around, I am reminded that if He could create, He can maintain. Again . . . I need only to stay in position. I need only to keep my hands empty of myself and my own ideas, apart from Him.

I have discovered with great relief that the Father is like Jesus Christ. I must confess that for more than a year after I became a Christian, there was deep unrest in my heart as I tried to conceive a bloodthirsty Father who was so selfish that He would not take me, His creation, without forcing His only Son to suffer on the cross. I am not ashamed to admit that these thoughts haunted my dreams at night and blocked my flow of words from more than one platform as I spoke, until a short time ago. I believed in the death of Jesus Christ on the cross, but I resented God the Father for it because I loved Jesus so much.

Now, I see at last that the cross is on the very heart of God, the Father. It is clear to me now that God Himself *was* in Christ reconciling the world unto Himself. He tries in every possible way to approach us in ways we can understand. He came to earth and confined Himself within the feeble frame of man, in order to make Himself more approachable to us. The Israelites understood the blood sacrifice. God gave Himself in a way His people could understand. He must remain true to His own holiness. And when we, by faith, receive His Son, we receive the Spirit of the Sacrificial Lamb as well.

I am filled with joy and peace to have discovered that God, the Father, is not a bloodthirsty power. He is one with Jesus Christ. He showed us His own loving nature by sending His Son. He said in essence: "I am like my Son." Jesus said: "I and my Father are one."

I am also overjoyed to have discovered that my Lord is a jealous God. That He wants me all to Himself. But I am relieved to find that His jealous nature is unlike ours. He is jealous for our own good. He created us, and only He knows how we will function best and find the greatest joy. He demands that we follow His laws, *not* because He is an ogre and a stern, relentless Being. He wants us to obey Him because only He knows our hearts and only He knows what is for our good. I am glad He is jealous and I am also glad I have discovered why He is jealous.

I am also glad I have discovered directly from my own experience with Christ that Christianity is *not* something foreign and strange and unnatural, which must be forced upon me if I am to live it successfully. I have discovered that when I received Jesus Christ and when His work of redemption became a reality in my own life, I was transformed, *restored* to that relaxed, natural, childlike state when man first walked in the garden with the Father in the cool of the evening and talked with Him as a child talks lovingly with his parent. I am a "new creature," at home with her God.

Finally, and most blessedly, I have come upon the happy moment of discovery that this life hid with Christ in God is a *continuous unfolding.* It is not a creed to which I pledge myself and between whose rigid confines I must from thenceforth march. This new life in Christ is to me an eternal beginning. A fresh moment by moment unfolding as I walk moment by moment in the very presence of the One to whom I belong. I find that as long as I am aware of His presence, I am adequate for any event.

To my great, glad amazement, I have discovered that I am His and He is mine — forever.